Debates in ESOL Teaching and Learning

Culture, communities and classrooms

Kathy Pitt

Routledge
Taylor & Francis Group

LONDON AND NEW YORK

First published 2005 by Routledge
2 Park Square, Milton Park, Abingdon, Oxon, OX14 4RN

Simultaneously published in the USA and Canada
by Routledge
270 Madison Ave, New York, NY 10016

Routledge is an imprint of the Taylor & Francis Group

Typeset in Baskerville by Keystroke, Jacaranda Lodge, Wolverhampton
Printed and bound in Great Britain by Cromwell Press, Trowbridge, Wiltshire

British Library Cataloguing in Publication Data
A catalogue record for this book is available from the British Library

Library of Congress Cataloging in Publication Data
Pitt, Kathy.
Debates in ESOL teaching and learning : culture, communities, and
classrooms / Kathy Pitt.
p. cm.
Includes bibliographical references and index.
1. English language–Study and teaching–Foreign speakers. 2. English
teachers–Training of. 3. Education, Bilingual–Teacher training. I. Title.

PE1128.A2P53 2005

428′.0071′1–dc22

2005002948

ISBN 0–415–35374–2 (hbk)
ISBN 0–415–35375–0 (pbk)

Contents

Series Editors' Preface

The books in this series are aimed mainly at teachers, trainers, researchers and postgraduate students concerned with the education of adults in the field of language, literacy and numeracy. They address people working and training teachers in the many contexts in which teaching and learning takes place: including colleges, family and community-based settings, workplaces and prisons. We expect the books to be useful within both initial and continuing professional development courses. They address the curriculum and subject specifications, as well as offering reflective and research dimensions for those whose interest has been sparked to probe deeper into the absorbing issues thrown up in the field. While recent national government strategies in the UK and some other countries have boosted research in the field and opportunities for professional development, as yet there are few easily available resources of the kind offered by the books in this series.

Each book in the series offers an up-to-date introduction to theory and research evidence in some aspect of the field, reviews the debates and issues and discusses how they apply to educational practice. The books are designed to be accessible to interested but non-specialist readers and each can be read independently as well as in relation to the series as a whole. The key readings and research evidence on which the books draw are international in origin and scope. Because of this and because they focus on topical debates and issues that are central to the field, the books will have wide appeal to the international research and practice community for adult literacy, language and numeracy. Development workers in a range of international contexts may also find them of interest.

These books draw on the authors' varied experience of teaching, researching and working with practitioners in short courses, summer schools, continuing professional development and networks. Each book reflects the approach of an individual author, and contains specially written discussion papers giving an overview of issues and debates, along with key readings brought together from a wide range of specialist sources. Each chapter has suggestions for exploring the material further, through reading, research activities and reflection. Key terms are explained throughout. These features, together with the access offered to key research articles in the field, make these books a unique, engaging, topic focussed resource for professional development.

As a whole, the series presents a coherent approach to literacy, numeracy and language as part of social and situated practice, seeing them as broader than simply skills to be acquired. In brief, the idea behind this approach is that literacy, numeracy and language are shaped by the social and cultural context within which they are embedded, the social relationships within which they happen, the meanings they have for users and the purposes they serve. This approach emphasises the importance of understanding the diversity of experience and knowledge that adults bring into formal learning situations and suggests ways of working in partnership with them to reflect and build on these resources in the curriculum. Over the last 15 years or so, this approach has produced some of the most exciting, leading edge thinking and research in the field and we are proud to be able to introduce this work to a wider audience and to demonstrate its relevance to policy and practice.

Debates in ESOL Teaching and Learning: Cultures, Communities and Classrooms addresses ESOL practitioners, teacher trainers and others who may be working with adult ESOL learners in their classes or who wish to gain a better understanding of what is known about adults learning a second or additional language. It offers an entry into the theory and research in the learning of English by speakers of other languages (ESOL) and offers an accessible discussion of contemporary and recent debates and research in this field.

The readings gathered together here reflect the diverse dimensions of adult additional language learning, ranging from work on cognitive processes, through the social contexts of language learning to issues connected with classroom cultures. This is a wide area, both geographically and socially. The research discussed in this book has been carried out in Europe, the USA, Canada and Australia. This research is about the learning by adult language learners in foreign language classrooms, by refugees and asylum seekers in ESOL classrooms and bilingual programmes and by migrant workers informally acquiring the dominant language of their new country.

The author, Kathy Pitt, writes from a broad experience of teaching English to speakers of other languages in a range of countries around the world. She brings her insights from this experience to bear on her discussion of the research presented here, ensuring that this book will have wide appeal internationally.

Acknowledgements

The author and the publishers wish to thank the following for permission to use copyright material. Every effort has been made to trace all the copyright holders, but if any have been inadvertently overlooked, the publishers will be pleased to make the necessary arrangement at the first opportunity.

Chapter 1

Reading 1 Multilingual Matters Ltd for extracts from Toshiyo Nabei Toshiyo and Merril Swain (2002) 'Learner awareness of recasts in classroom interaction: a case study of an adult EFL student's second language learning', *Language Awareness*, II, 1, pp. 47–50, 56–59

Reading 2 Routledge for extracts from Michael Breen (2001) 'The social context for language learning: a neglected situation?', in C. Candlin and N. Mercer (eds) *English Language Teaching in its Social Context: A Reader*, pp. 122–134

Chapter 2

Reading 1 TESOL Inc. for extracts from B. Norton and K. Toohey (2001) 'Changing perspectives on good language learners', *TESOL Quarterly* 35:2, pp. 307–310, 313–318

Reading 2 Longman for extracts from A. Chamot (2001) 'The role of learning strategies in second language acquisition', in M. Breen (ed.) *Learner Contributions to Language Learning: New Directions in Research*, pp. 25–35, 40–41

Chapter 3

Reading 1 Multilingual Matters Ltd for extracts from Mukul Saxena (1994) 'Literacies among the Panjabis in Southall (Britain)' in M. Hamilton, R. Barton and R. Ivanic (eds) *Worlds of Literacy*, section 1, pp. 195–200.

Reading 2 Routledge for extracts from David Crystal (2001) 'The future of Englishes', in A. Burns and C. Coffin (eds) *Analysing English in a Global Context: A Reader*, pp. 54–55, 55–56, 59–61

Reading 3 Jane McLaughlin for (1986) 'Developing writing in English from mother-tongue storytelling', *Language Issues* 1, pp. 31–34

Chapter 4

Reading 1 Oxford University Press for extracts from Richard Kern (2000) 'Linguistic resources: Writing systems and media', *Literacy and Language Teaching*, pp. 68–74

Reading 2 TESOL Inc. for extracts from Jill Sinclair Bell (1995) 'The relationship between L1 and L2 literacy: some complicating factors', *TESOL Quarterly* 29: 4, pp. 691–702

Reading 3 Lawrence Erlbaum Associates for extracts from Elsa Auerbach (1996) *From the Community to the Community: A Guidebook for Participatory Literacy Training*, pp. 9–12, 16–18

Chapter 5

Reading 1 Oxford University Press for extracts from Ronald Carter (1998) 'Orders of reality: CANCODE, communication, and culture', *ELT Journal* 52:1, pp. 43–53

Reading 2 Longman for extracts from K. Bremer *et al.* (1996) 'Case studies: the making of understanding in extended interactions', in K. Bremer *et al. Achieving Understanding: Discourse in Intercultural Encounters* pp. 110–117, 145–146, 151–154, 156–158

Introduction

What this book is about

This book provides an entry into the field of theory and research into adult learning of additional languages, especially the learning of English by speakers of other languages (ESOL). It is for ESOL practitioners. This field of theory and research is a wide one, both geographically and socially. Research discussed in this book has been carried out in Europe, the USA, Canada and Australia. This research is about students who are learning in foreign language classrooms, refugees and asylum seekers in ESOL classrooms, and bilingual programmes and migrant workers informally acquiring the dominant language of their new country.

Although much of the research discussed has been carried out in other countries, this book has been written with particular learners in mind: those adults in the UK who need English for the workplace, for study in further and higher education, and for living in the community. These learners are not, of course, a homogeneous group of people. They are made up of adults from settled communities of immigrants from the new Commonwealth and the more fluctuating populations of refugees, asylum seekers and migrant workers. Their reasons for being here are many, as are their circumstances, and their experiences of spoken and written language use and formal learning are also diverse. Many have professional backgrounds; some have had practically no formal education (see Thompson 1994; Schellekens 2001).

This diversity is a key dimension to the exploration of language learning in this book. It links to debates about the nature of additional language learning. What are the relationships between the mental processes involved in language learning and the socially and culturally situated contexts of learning? This question threads through all of the chapters, and much of the research discussed or included as readings attempts to address it in one form or another.

There are three main themes that run through this book. First, the learners and the language learning process are at the centre of all discussions. Second, as most of these learners come to formal ESOL provision for help, and this book is written for ESOL professionals who provide this support, the nature of learning in the ESOL classroom is another focus. Third, the relationship between teaching and learning is another issue that weaves through the chapters, bringing in discussion of types of classroom tasks and language teaching methodologies.

Both learning and teaching are, of course, shaped by educational and other government policies. At the time of writing this book British government policy on new refugees and asylum seekers is one of dispersal throughout England and Wales. Individuals in these categories may be moved without much notice as their official status and rights to benefits change. Such a policy presents obvious difficulties for those refugees and asylum seekers who are learning English, and for their teachers.

Educational policy has also changed a great deal over the past decade, including the bringing together of Adult Basic Education (ABE) and ESOL provision in Further Education colleges and the introduction of a core curriculum. What have not changed are assumptions underlying polices about the monolingual and monocultural nature of the state (except in Wales), and a lack of recognition and support for community languages. The findings of the research, and the differing approaches to teaching language and literacy that are explored in this book, sometimes run counter to present policies, and readers are encouraged to reflect on and discuss these tensions in the activities at the end of each chapter.

The book starts in Chapter 1 with an overview of some of the key concepts that have emerged from almost fifty years of research into second language acquisition (SLA). Much of this research has not been concerned with adult ESOL learners and contexts. However, theories and findings from this field of study are often applied to ESOL learning contexts, and specific research centring on ESOL adult learners is a more recent phenomenon. An overarching question in this first chapter is: What can we learn from *any* study of additional language learning? How crucial are the social and cultural differences between learners and contexts?

In Chapter 2 the focus switches from studies attempting to capture the general process of language learning explored in Chapter 1 to the individual nature of learning. Many SLA studies have attempted to find out what makes a 'good' language learner. We look at some of this research and compare it with research that focuses specifically on ESOL learners, and argue that social factors are as significant as individual learning strategies.

Chapter 3 aims to widen the discussion on language learning by exploring a dimension of language use that is missing from much of the research and theory discussed in the first two chapters, namely multilingualism. People often move between two or three languages on a daily basis, and their language choices are bound up with their feelings and their social identities. This chapter critiques the often taken-for-granted monolingual assumptions underlying much research into additional language learning and discusses bilingual language methodologies.

The final two chapters are dedicated to issues surrounding the two modes of language use: oral and written. First, in Chapter 4 the focus is on literacy learning. Here the issues are both about the social and the cultural nature of literacy, and the learning needs of those learners who have little or no experience of using any written languages. In the final chapter the focus turns back to oral communication, which has been the main focus of studies discussed in the first three chapters. Chapter 5 explores the relationships between the teaching of spoken English in the classroom and the often uncomfortable and unequal interactions in English that ESOL learners have to cope with outside the classroom.

This exploration of the learning of spoken English takes us back full circle to the discussions about language learning in the first two chapters. Chapter 5 takes us back to Chapter 1. Overall, the book has to be laid out in a line, with a beginning and an end, and distinct chapters, because of the writing medium used. However, all research into, and thinking about, learning and teaching is interconnected. The discussions in each chapter are only one part of a whole network or web of ideas, explorations and debates.

How to use this book

The book consists of five chapters. Each chapter is accompanied by two or three readings that extend or exemplify the points discussed in the main text. These readings are extracts from research or theoretical papers. The guided reading activities that you will find within each chapter are there to suggest a reading path through these extracts which ties in with the main discussion. The questions aim to give a focus to your reading.

At the end of each chapter there are discussion activities based on the main text and the readings. There is also a practical research activity linked to the issues of each chapter. These activities are designed to engage you further with research and theoretical issues around additional language learning, and to enable you to bring your own professional experience to these debates.

References

Schellekens, P. (2001) *English Language as a Barrier to Employment, Training and Education*, London, DFEE.

Thompson, J. (1994) 'Developing an English for Academic and Professional Purposes Programme for refugees/asylum seekers', *Language Issues* 6: 2, pp. 29–32.

Some useful journals

Journal of Applied Linguistics
Language and Education
Language Issues (NATECLA)
Language Learning
Language Teaching Research
TESOL Quarterly

Some useful websites

Canadian Centre for Victims of Torture (CCVT)
http://www.icomm.ca/ccvt

National Association for Teachers of English and other Community Languages to Adults
http://www.natecla.org.uk/

National Research and Development Centre for Adult Literacy and Numeracy
http://www.nrdc.org.uk

Refugee Council
http://www.refugeecouncil.org.uk/

Chapter I

Learning an additional language

Looking for universal characteristics

Introduction

This chapter begins with a whole series of studies and discussions, called second language acquisition (SLA). SLA researchers have often studied foreign language classrooms or the second language learning of children – learners and contexts that may seem very distant from the adult ESOL learners in your classrooms. However, these studies have been the source of significant theories that form part of the foundation of current research into additional language learning. In addition, much of the research and discussion about ESOL learning today assumes a knowledge of concepts that have arisen from attempts to identify and explain universal characteristics of second language acquisition. Thus in the first section of this chapter we briefly describe some of these key concepts, in order to help you to understand current research and theory.

In the second section we look at three examples of research into additional language learning that have focused on language classrooms. They have been chosen for three reasons. First, they focus on learning in classrooms, and most ESOL provision supports language learning in this context. Second, they illustrate the different approaches to classroom research discussed by Michael Breen in the second reading of this chapter. Finally, they have been chosen to help us appreciate the difficulties of tracing such a complex process.

Claims to knowledge in this area usually attract debate and critique. Much of this arises because of the need to cross traditional research boundaries in order to try to understand additional and foreign language learning. To understand the acquisition process involves, among other factors, knowledge about mental processes (cognition), about the learning context and social relations, and about how language actually operates in social practice. Thus studies by researchers expert in the way the mind works (that is, in cognitive processes such as remembering) are accused of neglecting the social situation of the learner, and those who have studied classroom relationships, or the language experiences of migrant workers, are criticized for neglecting specific cognitive processes. It is very difficult for specific research projects to cover all aspects of language acquisition.

Therefore, many questions about this language learning process remain unanswered. However, second language acquisition studies help us to understand the complexity of the process and the variables involved, so we start this chapter with some of the key concepts that have emerged both from this research activity and theoretical perspectives (for a detailed overview of SLA studies see Ellis, 2001; Firth and Wagner, 1997; Long, 1988; Mitchell and Myles, 2001).

Key concepts of SLA

This section aims to give you a brief introduction to some of the terms and ideas that you will meet when reading about SLA research and theory.

Interlanguage

Much of the earlier research in SLA was inspired by advances in knowledge of how children acquire their first language. In these first language acquisition studies investigations of the speech of young children showed that children developed their understanding and use of grammatical structures, such as negatives and inter-rogatives, in a particular order. It was argued that deviant grammatical forms produced by children (such as 'I goed to the park') were evidence of a subconscious but active mental learning process whereby children were producing speech on the basis of their current knowledge of the rules. In this example the child has overgeneralized the rule about forming the past tense by applying it incorrectly to an irregular verb.

Consequently, researchers set out to study the language produced by learners of additional and foreign languages to see if there was any similarity between first and second language acquisition. Obviously, all additional language learners produce incorrect forms when they speak, partly because of their lack of knowledge of the grammar of the new language, and partly because their knowledge of their first language can lead them to hypothesize incorrectly about similarities in struc-ture. However, would a study of learner language over time show systematic and patterned changes in the errors made that could indicate an active universal process, despite differences caused by first language interference?

At first, these studies did indeed indicate the possibility of there being an order in the acquisition of certain structural features universal to all learners of second languages. But this was an enormous task to carry out, and convincing evidence has not emerged.

What these studies of learner language did do, however, was to establish the concept of a dynamic and systematic process of language learning, and the language produced by learners as they learn was given the name *interlanguage* (often abbreviated to IL) to reflect this process. The errors made by learners as they developed their knowledge of the new language were characteristic of inter-language and seen as part of this active process. This way of thinking about errors opposed the previously dominant behaviourist thinking about second language acquisition. For behaviourists, learner errors were due to poor learning or bad habits, because learning was solely a process of repetition, imitation and memorization. Whereas, for these interlanguage theorists, errors were evidence of an active internal learning process: 'Learners work their way through a number of *developmental stages*, from very primitive and deviant versions of the L2, to progressively more elaborate and target-like versions' (Mitchell and Myles, 2001, p. 18, emphasis in original). Thus the word *interlanguage* was coined to show that learners are actively journeying from one language to another in the learning process, and that their errors are part of this journey.

Comprehensible input

Making comparisons between first and second language acquisition led some researchers to hypothesize that additional language learners needed conditions for learning similar to those of first language acquisition. Young children gradually acquire the full range of grammatical structures through immersion in the language but without being formally taught. It was therefore argued that additional language learners also need to be exposed to language that is meaningful to them in order to learn a language. This meaningful language was called *comprehensible input*. The theories of Stephen Krashen on the role of input were both the most extreme and the most well known (Krashen, 1985). For Krashen, input which is at the right level of difficulty for the learner is all that is needed for interlanguage development and change. He points to the successes achieved by immersion education for children (for example, Canadian English-speaking children are taught school subjects in French) as instances of learning through comprehensible input. In this type of education there is little formal second language teaching.

Output

There have been many critiques of Krashen's language learning hypotheses (e.g. McLaughlin, 1987; Skehan, 2001; and see both readings for this unit). Some of the criticism has centred on the evidence from SLA research into immersion education. Although earlier studies of additional language learning through immersion showed that children's additional language level was much higher than those who learned the language in formal language classrooms, these earlier studies focused on learners' abilities to comprehend the target language. Later studies of Canadian immersion programmes showed a gap between the children's understanding of the target language and their production of the language (Swain and Lapkin, 1982). This led Merrill Swain to argue that the act of speaking – *output* – was also a necessary condition for interlanguage development (Swain, 1995). She hypothesized that having to interact helped learners to make the input more comprehensible, and also compelled learners to pay attention to the role of grammar in the input and to try out hypotheses gained in the learning process.

Cognitive processes: information processing and restructuring

Output is also considered essential to language learning by those researchers who have focused on trying to understand the mental processes involved in language learning (see e.g. Johnson, 1996; Skehan, 2001). Cognitive psychologists have attempted to explore what happens when we listen to or read something in the additional language, and when we speak or write with it. This is generally referred to as *information processing*. They stress that both comprehension and production are complex multi-level tasks. Speaking, for example, involves:

- Deciding on the content of the verbal message. This draws on the speaker's knowledge of the topic and of the interactional conventions in which she is participating.
- Formulating the content. This draws on her current knowledge of vocabulary and grammar.
- Preparing how to articulate the content. This draws on her knowledge of the sound system.
- Actually producing the sounds, plus appropriate stress and intonation.

Throughout these phases the speaker also continually monitors her selection for appropriateness and accuracy. Over time, and given the opportunities, the learner is able to reduce the amount of processing time she needs to speak through the creation of automatic links between the different processes.

Changes in a learner's grammatical or lexical knowledge are called *restructuring* because new knowledge can cause the learner to revise her previously learned knowledge. Such restructuring can have an effect on information processing. Although new linguistic knowledge may result in greater accuracy or complexity of speech, the new knowledge can also seem to slow the learner down if this new item causes change within the existing knowledge store.

Acquisition versus learning

Krashen argued that learning an additional language was parallel to learning a first language in that it was a subconscious process and that formal teaching of structure did not help. Here is an example of this first language acquisition process that focuses on the acquisition of English language negatives. Young children start off by adding the word *No* to the beginning of utterances ('No comb hair') and then gradually change to embedding *no* within the clause, before the verb ('Daddy no comb hair'). The correct use of negative modal verbs (e.g. *can't*) come later. Children are not usually aware of making these changes, or of how they came about, and resist correction by adults. Thus Krashen talks of *acquisition* processes rather than conscious *learning*. This view challenges the usefulness of the teaching of grammatical structures in language classrooms.

However, direct comparisons between older children and adults learning an additional language and young children learning a first language do not take into account the huge differences in knowledge of the world and variety of learning experiences between these groups of learners, let alone the fact that young children are developing their cognitive processes alongside their linguistic abilities. Furthermore, it has since been argued that learning an additional language involves the conscious process of *noticing*. This is a process whereby the learner consciously notices a difference or 'gap' between her additional language use (or interlanguage) and that of the text she is reading or the person she is talking to. This provides an opportunity for a change in her knowledge of the language (restructuring). Noticing is said to be an action that comes from the learner when, and if, she is ready. This learning may be implicit, in that the learner may not stop in the middle of an interaction and reflect on this new knowledge. If questioned, however, the learner can explain her change in language production (see Ellis (2001) for more information on noticing).

It is argued that knowledge of the form of an additional language, usually gained through the language classroom, can support this process of noticing, and therefore, contrary to Krashen's theories, formal learning can play a significant role in the process.

Socialization

More recently, some researchers have highlighted the social nature of additional language learning, and suggest that we should talk about *socialization* rather than acquisition, because learners need to learn about the social and cultural conventions of language use as well as the structures and vocabulary. This emphasis has come from studies of minority language workers' language use in naturally occurring situations in the target culture (Bremer *et al.*, 1996). These studies show that minority language workers develop the majority language through having to use it to pursue their daily lives, for example, in the workplace, or while looking for work. (We discuss such research in more detail in Chapters 2 and 5.)

An example of such learning is given by Celia Roberts in the box below. It is the closing moments of an interview between a job counsellor (T) and Marcello (M), an Italian worker in Germany who is seeking employment:

---

1 *M*: Wir muss vergessen \<laughs>
    We have to forget
2 *T*: Ja + gut + dann hatten wir die saache für heut
    OK good so we're through for today
3   Und wenn sie also in zukunft noch fragen haben kommen sie bei mir vorbei ja
    And if you have any questions in future you'll look in OK

> 4 *M:* Ja
>   *Yes*
> 5 *T:* <Rufen sie an> ok <leans, back, speaks quietly, looks at door, stands up>
>   *Give me a call OK*
> 6 *M:* So und jetzt muss ich gehen
>   *So and now I must go*
> 7 *T:* <Ja>
> 8 *M:* < > <both laugh>
> 9 *T:* Wiedersehen
>   *Bye*
> 10 *M:* Wiedersehen danke
>   *Bye thank you*
>
> Transcript conventions
> +   short pause
> < >   additional comments on way of speaking, etc.
> [ ]   overlap
> (xxx)   inaudible or omitted word
>
> At one level, this could be construed as a simple case of pragmatic failure. Marcello fails to understand the pre-closing signals of T including 'ja', 'gut' and 'dann hatten wir die sache für hurt' and advice for the future. It is only with the nonverbal cues that Marcello realizes that they are in the middle of leave taking. His interpretive difficulty is not surprising since as Scarcella (1982) has argued, conventional features such as greetings are acquired before pre-closing. But this sequence is also an unusually explicit moment of language socialization when at line 6 Marcello topicalizes the act of departure. This is more than just a matter of picking up on some pre-closing signals, and it is worth mentioning here that the crucial nonverbal signals which are part of the interactive environment are rarely considered in linguistic pragmatics.
>
> (C. Roberts, in Candlin and Mercer, 2001: 111)

At line 6 Marcello actually makes explicit his new understanding of the meaning of both linguistic and nonverbal signals that the interview is over. Roberts calls this process an *apprenticeship model*, where the learner learns by doing, by participating in social interactions. However, she also points out that this model does not take into account social factors that affect learning, such as class and identity. These are discussed in Chapter 2.

Although these concepts have been introduced here in roughly the order they were developed, they do not represent a neat set of 'steps' in the process of understanding how we learn another language. Specific research projects tend to draw on only one or two dimensions of this field of work, depending on their interests and the types of research methodologies they are using.

In the following section we move on to look at three small pieces of research that have all focused on learning in the language classroom, but have asked different questions and so have used different methods of investigation. These studies illustrate the critique of SLA classroom research offered by Breen in Reading 2, and so are also intended to help you evaluate his arguments. I suggest you read this section before reading Breen. The first piece of research approximates to what Breen calls 'the classroom as experimental laboratory' and the second study is an example of his category of 'the classroom as discourse'. The third piece of research attempts to bring together the methods of these two different approaches in order to try to investigate both cognitive processes and the social nature of learning. This attempt to chart the relationships between the mental processing of new language and the social relations of a class is essential to understanding language learning in classrooms, according to Breen.

Research into language learning in the classroom: some examples

As may be seen in the above section on acquisition versus learning, the role of the language classroom in additional language learning has been both argued for and argued against. Since ESOL teachers have little choice but to support additional language learning from within the classroom, we will now look at three studies that attempt to investigate the thorny question of the relationship between teaching and learning. The third study is described in detail in the first reading of this chapter, so it is summarized only briefly in this section.

Tracing uptake

The first piece of research we shall look at was carried out in a foreign language classroom. It is included here because it addresses the important question of the relationship between classroom practice and student learning. The research was undertaken in one class by Assia Slimani in Algeria (Slimani, 2001). Her aim was to record what learners claimed to have learned from a particular lesson, which she called *uptake*, and then to analyse how these claims related to classroom interaction. Thus the research relies on the recall of the learners, who were thirteen male Algerian students studying engineering at the beginning of their first year at university. They all spoke both Arabic and French and were on a six-month intensive English language programme to prepare them to study engineering in English. The class used in the research was teacher-centred, and focused on presentation of structure and practice of this through textbook exercises.

Slimani observed and audio-recorded this class for two hours a week during the first six weeks of term. At the end of each of these observed classes the learners filled in a questionnaire asking them to relate in detail, in terms of grammar, words and expressions, pronunciation and spelling, what they recalled from the events of the lesson in which they had just participated. After about three hours they were given back their filled-in uptake questionnaires and asked to record what they thought they had newly learned in that day's lesson and what they had encountered in previous lessons or with different teachers. They could also add more uptake if necessary. This delay was to allow the learners time to absorb what they thought they had learned. All the questionnaires were in French, as were the two interviews which Slimani also held with each learner during the observation period. During the interviews Slimani tried to find out the reasons why the learners thought they had learned something new.

On analysing the questionnaires and the lesson transcripts, Slimani found that most of the claims for new learning consisted of lexical items. She argued that this focus on vocabulary could have resulted from the fact that most of the structural items presented by the teacher were also part of the high school English curriculum, so the students had probably already been taught them. She found that the majority of these items claimed to have been learned had, in one way or another, been the topic of conversation during the class (112 out of the 126). What she meant was that each item had had their meaning and/or spelling and/or pronunciation discussed by the teacher and/or learners. Many of these items were not part of the teacher's plan but arose incidentally during the class. However, of the language points specifically focused on by the teacher as part of his plan, only 44 per cent were claimed as being newly learned by the learners. Since this was a traditional teacher-centred grammar class, the teacher initiated most of the topics in the interaction. Yet the rare occasions when the learners initiated a topic (less than a quarter of the class time) resulted in more claims for uptake than those initiated by the teacher.

Even though learner participation in this class was limited, the fact that most of the uptake resulted from discussion and explanation points towards a positive role for the conscious exploration of language structure. Most of the unnoticed items (present in the transcripts but not referred to in the questionnaires) were instances of error treatment by the teacher. Slimani noted that the teacher's treatment of error was erratic, but also hypothesized that the failure to learn from error correction could result from the learners not being ready to internalize the correct form. This hypothesis draws on the concept of interlanguage.

Slimani also found that uptake was highly idiosyncratic. Almost 75 per cent of the total number of claims were reported by no more than three learners at a time and 37 per cent were reported by only one learner. Only a tiny number of the claims (3 per cent) were made by nine or more learners. This suggests that learning is also an individual process, as we explore in Chapter 2. It was not possible, within this project, to investigate the learners' retention and production of this uptake in the long term.

Error treatment and learner response

Some classroom studies focus on investigating and describing particular patterns of classroom interaction that may or may not contribute towards language learning. One such study was carried out in four French primary immersion classes where French is the main medium for the classroom regardless of the pupils' home language (Lyster and Ranta, 1997). The aim is that those pupils whose home language is English acquire the additional language through general primary education which includes, of course, instruction in reading and writing in French. This study is one of many that focus on the teacher treatment of errors through analysis of classroom discourse. The moment when a teacher corrects an error made by a learner is an easily identifiable opportunity for learning to take place, and so many researchers have tried to explore and understand these particular interactions.

The study is also of interest, since its context, immersion education, is said to be one of the ideal approaches to communicative language teaching; a methodology that emphasizes the role of meaningful interaction between language learners. This methodology currently dominates language pedagogy and materials worldwide.

In this particular study of error correction 18.3 hours of lessons, conducted by four teachers, were audio-recorded. These lessons included subject matter classes, such as science and maths and French language arts classes focusing on reading, writing and discussion. The transcripts were then analysed to trace the different types of corrective feedback used by the teachers and the learners' uptake, or lack of uptake, of these. (Note that, confusingly, the researchers here are using the notion of *uptake* differently from Slimani. Lyster and Ranta use the word *uptake* to mean that a learner has recognized that the teacher's speech is intended to be a correction of an error.)

As a result of the analysis, six types of teacher feedback were identified:

1   *Explicit correction*
    The teacher provides the correct form and makes it clear that what the learner has said is incorrect (e.g. by saying 'You should say').
2   *Recasts*
    The teacher reformulates all or part of the learner's utterance using correct forms. These are generally implicit in that they are not introduced by phrases such as 'You mean'.
3   *Clarification requests*
    The teacher indicates that she does not understand the learner's utterance.
4   *Metalinguistic feedback*
    The teacher indicates there is a problem with the utterance, and points to the nature of the problem without giving the correct form (e.g. by saying 'Can you find your mistake?').
5   *Elicitation*
    The teacher asks learners to complete the teacher's sentence, or asks questions

such as 'How do we say xx in French?', or asks learners to reformulate their utterance.

6   *Repetition*
     The teacher repeats the learner's error, often using intonation to highlight it.

Some of these different types were used in combination.

On examining the transcripts, Lyster and Ranta found that one-third of all student turns contained at least one error, but only 62 per cent of these errors were corrected in some way by the teacher. Fifty-five per cent of these teacher corrections or feedback resulted in learner uptake; that is, the learner realized the teacher was reacting to an error the learner had made. However, this uptake only resulted in learners trying to correct what they said (called repair) in 27 per cent of the turns. The most frequently used type of error correction used by the teacher was recast (55 per cent of all feedback). However, recast was the least likely to result in a corrected form of the error, while elicitation and metalinguistic feedback were the most successful.

Lyster later argued that the learning situation of these students may have contributed to the failure of recasts to result in uptake or learner correction. Since the emphasis of the immersion classroom is on meaning rather than language form, he suggests that the learners may assume that the teacher is responding to the content of what they are saying (their utterances) when they make a recast. In situations in which the negotiation of meaning is the primary goal, it is more difficult for learners to actively learn from input. Minority language workers using the additional language in bureaucratic encounters such as interviews with government officials are in similar situations to the learners in this study, and research into their informal learning is discussed in Chapter 5.

What this study shows is the variety of ways error treatment is carried out by teachers, and also that many of the learners' errors were not given feedback, or were given feedback that did not appear helpful to the learner. What such a study cannot do is explore why each instance of feedback is helpful or unhelpful from a particular learner's perspective. A much smaller scale study in Japan attempted to do just that.

📖 *Activity: Guided Reading*

Reading I:

Nabei, T. and Swain, M. (2002) 'Learner awareness of recasts in classroom inter-
    action: a case study of an adult EFL student's second language learning', *Language
    Awareness* II: 1, pp. 47–50, 56–59.

The third piece of research is the subject of the first reading. It is an intensive study focusing on just one Japanese learner of English in a language

classroom in Japan and her learning from a teacher's use of recast. The learner's participation in a discussion class was observed and videotaped six times. Within a week of each class the student did a test based on the language points that had been focused on in teacher recasts of learner errors. This test asked the student to judge whether or not sentences were grammatically correct, and to indicate how sure she was. This is called a *grammaticality test*. The student then watched the recorded classroom interaction and talked about what was going on inside her mind during teacher feedback. This research procedure is called *stimulated recall*. The student was also given an overall test about three weeks after the final interview.

Now read the extracts from the article reporting this research:

> Do you think the methodology and findings of this research are relevant to ESOL contexts and learners?

The study

The present case study of a L2 learner, Shoko, was conducted to investigate this Japanese EFL college student's awareness of recast feedback provided by the teacher in a theme-based English classroom. We were concerned with how recasts were provided, what Shoko learned from them, and how Shoko reacted to them. We elicited Shoko's awareness – often not observable in her behaviour in the class – through stimulated recall. Specifically, the research questions we address in this study are:

1.   What opportunities did Shoko have to hear recasts from the teacher?
2.   What was Shoko's awareness of the teacher's recasts?
3.   What connections are there among the teacher recasts, Shoko's awareness and her learning?

The student

Shoko was a 19-year-old college student in Japan. Being interested in communicating in English, she took and passed the entrance examination to a private women's college specialising in English education, and was placed in the upper-intermediate level according to the placement test the college administered at the beginning of the school year.

Shoko was an active and motivated English learner. While in high school, she found communicating in English fascinating and attended a private English conversation school for a year. She spent two weeks home – staying in Canada during the summer vacation between the first and second semesters of her first college year. She also had a Canadian boyfriend during the period the research was conducted.

She liked watching English movies and TV shows. 'Beverly Hills 90201' was one of her favourites; according to her self-report, she watched the show in English and 'enjoyed its feeling' (Interview 3; 19 Oct.).

The classroom

The English Discussion Course in this college curriculum was one of the five compulsory English courses for the first-year students: English Grammar, Phonetics, Reading, Academic Writing, and English Discussion. The latter three courses aimed to increase students' ability to use the language skilfully by providing them with academic themes for using English in context.

The Discussion Course especially emphasised developing fluency in English oral communication. Living in an EFL context (i.e. having few opportunities or needs to communicate in English on a daily basis) and having learned English in traditional teacher-fronted classrooms in high school, the students were, in general, hesitant in expressing themselves in English. Thus, they were expected to improve their communication skills through discussing themes such as 'human rights' and 'environmental issues' during the two terms the course was offered. The students were also expected to 'understand and use the vocabulary of the topics with a fair degree of accuracy' as well as 'to expand their horizons' to become aware of current events in the society and world (College Catalogue: 16). The course textbook contained many communicative activities, such as information gap and ranking tasks, interviews and surveys to facilitate students' discussion. The class met twice a week for 70 minutes each time for 10 weeks in the first and second terms.

Shoko's Discussion Course was composed of 28 young women, all first-year students, and an American EFL teacher. The students, 18 to 20 years old, were also placed in this course according to placement test results. Ms Johnson was an experienced teacher who had taught English for more than 10 years in Japan. She encouraged students to speak in English all the time in class. In order to maximise the students' opportunities to use English as well as to make her interaction with students more feasible, Ms Johnson adopted a group-work strategy in her teaching (Interview 10; Sept). She grouped her students into seven groups of four, and most activities were assigned as group work. She monitored the students' use of English in group activities, and any group that extensively used Japanese was sometimes penalised: classroom participation points were deducted.

General procedures

The research involved cycles of a set procedure. A basic cycle was composed of (1) classroom observation and videotaping of a 70-minute class period, (2) administration of a Grammaticality Judgement (GJ) test (Test 1) within a week of the videotaping, followed by (3) a stimulated recall interview with Shoko. This cycle was conducted approximately each week and was repeated six times from the third to eighth week within the 10-week term. Additionally, a GJ test (Test 2) composed of all the previously given GJ tests was administered after the term was completed (approximately three weeks after the last cycle).

During the classroom observation, one of the researchers (the first author) was in the back of the room and a video camera was set to capture Shoko and her group members' dialogues and activities. A multi-direction microphone was also set up at the centre of the group table. The taped dialogue was transcribed and analysed for recast episodes (RE). (A full description of REs is provided in the next section.) The REs identified during the class period were the database for the test and the 'stimuli' for the interview for that cycle.

. . .

After completing the test, a stimulated recall interview based on the videotape was conducted. Scenes of classroom and group activities involving recasts were shown and Shoko was asked to recall and tell what she was thinking at that moment. The baseline question was 'what were you thinking then?' A few episodes of other types of feedback and other activity moments were also shown as distracters. The interviews were conducted in Japanese since the information Shoko was asked to deliver was complex. Shoko's verbal reports were audiotaped and later transcribed for analyses.

Stimulated recall is an introspective method, based on an information-processing approach. This method is recognised as a means to explore L2 learning processes which otherwise are not observable (Cohen, 1987; Færch and Kasper, 1987). In stimulated recall, prompts such as audio- or videotaped events are used to stimulate the participants' recall of their mental processes during the events. This method and the theoretical rationale for its use are outlined in detail in Gass and Mackey (2000).

Data analyses

The data consisted of REs identified in the classroom discourse, Shoko's verbal reports from the stimulated recall interviews, and GJ test results.

Recasts and recast episodes

A recast in this study was operationally defined as either an isolated or expanded rephrasing of learners' non-target-like utterances provided by the teacher imme-diately after the non-target-like utterances. Non-target-like utterances are those with linguistic problems (i.e. morpho-syntactic, lexical, phonological) (e.g. Lyster, 1998b), use of L1 (e.g. Lyster & Ranta, 1997), incomplete and fragmented utterances (e.g. Farrar, 1990, 1992), or combinations of these problems. Unlike previous recast studies, we allowed for relatively diverse problem areas for which recasts could be provided, reflecting actual occurrences of recasts in natural classroom inter-action.

A recast episode (RE) was defined as a sequence of one or more feedback turns, involving at least one recast, to deal with one aspect of non-target-like language use found in a learner's utterance. This is a sub-category of 'Error Treatment Episode' (ETE) in which a non-target-like utterance was reacted to by an interlocutor in any form of feedback (i.e. recast, explicit correction, metalinguistic feedback, elicitation, clarification request, or repetition as in Lyster and Ranta, 1997). An episode starts with a non-target-like utterance which is reacted to by an interlocutor, and ends when feedback ends and the topic shifts. A RE may contain a single recasting treatment (i.e. Single Recast Episode [SRE]) as in Example 1. In this episode, the teacher gave an expanded recast in response to Shoko's non-target-like utterance, and moved on to the next topic thus ending the episode.

Example 1:

5B–016 **Teacher:**   OK. Everything was on sale. Why?

5B–017 **Shoko:**   Because . . . baseball winner.

5B–018 **Teacher:**   OK. Because they won the Japan series. Do you like baseball?

A RE may contain more than one recast as in Example 2, which is a compound recast episode (CPRE). In this example, the teacher provided two isolated recasts, initially to complete the student's utterance (line 3A–471), and to correct the phrase constructed (line 3A–473).

Example 2:

3A–469 **Teacher:**   OK. Masako?

3A–470 **Masako:**   Studying hard to en- . . . ent . . .

3A–471 **Teacher:**   Enter

3A–472 **Masako:**   enter examination

3A–473 **Teacher:**   OK. Studying hard for examinations. OK. That's a problem, yeah.

A RE may also contain other forms of feedback as in Example 3, which is a complex recast episode (CXRE). In this example, the teacher put Asako's problematic sentence into a more target-form and added contrastive explanations of usage (i.e. explicit correction).

Example 3:

6A–004 **Asako:**   (snip) . . . My opinion is . . . cats are more dangerous animal than dog because they . . . they keep going when they met a car. They never change their way, and they . . . run over.

6A–005 **Teacher:**   OK. Yeah, . . . cats are . . . Cats are at more danger. OK. So something is dangerous is going to hurt something else. At danger is they can be hurt. OK.

Discussion

Some findings in this case study are consistent with those found in previous recast studies, and others are different. We discuss these findings under three topics: description of recast feedback in Shoko's classroom; Shoko's reaction to recasts; and effectiveness of recasts as corrective feedback.

Recasts in Shoko's classroom

The outstanding difference about recasts in this classroom from other classroom-based feedback research was the infrequency of teacher recasts to which Shoko was exposed. In fact, teacher feedback in general was extremely infrequent: only 23 REs within the 420 minutes of recording time. This finding suggests that teacher feedback practice is greatly influenced by the teaching context.

Ms Johnson's feedback strategies appeared to be influenced by the school curriculum and syllabi. In contrast to the FL classrooms studied in previous recast studies (e.g. Ohta, 2000), Ms Johnson placed little emphasis on the instruction of linguistic components. This was probably because she knew her students were concurrently taking classes which had a more linguistic orientation, such as Grammar, Phonology and Academic Writing. Ms Johnson prioritised 'facilitation of discussion' to 'linguistic correction' in her time-constrained class because the curriculum required only 'a fair degree of accuracy' (College Catalogue: 16).

Another possible explanation for the infrequent recast feedback is the teacher's familiarity with teaching English in Japan. Having taught English to Japanese learners for more than ten years and being also a fluent speaker of Japanese herself, Ms Johnson was familiar with Japanese students' linguistic problems, such as L1-transferred errors and strong Japanese accents, and did not have much difficulty inferring her students' meaning. Thus, she did not need to make frequent negotiation moves. Mackey *et al.* (2000) provided a similar explanation for their findings that the near-native Italian as FL interlocutor interacting with the IFL (Italian as a Foreign Language) students did not provide as frequent phonological recasts as the NS interlocutors did to their ESL learners. The researchers thought this was because the near-native interlocutor was familiar with the IFL students' phonological problems and thus had fewer comprehension difficulties.

Despite this outstanding difference regarding teacher feedback, the recasts in Shoko's classroom were discovered to share many characteristics found in the previous studies. Recasting was the feedback move most frequently employed by the teacher. As in studies by Lyster (1998b) and Mackey et al. (2000), recasts in this classroom were also provided more to grammatical than to lexical errors. As discussed by Oliver (1995) and Lyster (1998a), teacher recasts were also not likely to provide opportunities for students to repair.

Shoko's reaction to recasts

Shoko's reactions to recasts were not simply determined by the linguistic elements of input (e.g. grammar vs. lexicon, isolated vs. expanded modification). They were also influenced by the conversational context and her awareness. Shoko's stimulated recall revealed that she was an active communicator. She was motivated to understand and be understood by others during English conversation. . . . When she was engaged in the conversation, and felt meaning was important and relevant, Shoko actively and reflectively listened to the conversation.

Shoko's active and reflective listening was often analytically oriented. Her sensitivity and awareness toward her peers' as well as her own language use was evident. . . . Shoko naturally '[stood] away, so to speak, from the language in use [and] examine[d] it' during meaningful interaction (Stern, 1990: 98). Her observation and identification of language-related problems enabled her to notice teacher recasts, with which she compared the language forms in question. Because small group interaction was more directly engaging, Shoko was more likely to notice teacher feedback in the group contexts than teacher-fronted interaction.

Effectiveness of recasts

In general, the teacher's recasts did not contribute a great deal to Shoko's immediate learning of the language. However, detailed analyses of REs in relation to Shoko's awareness and test results show some tendencies. First, the recast could become contextually explicit depending on the way the teacher provided it. As seen in Table 1, three REs looked very similar according to Lyster's (1998a) descriptive categories, but had different impacts on Shoko. In Episodes 1102, 1106, and 108, the teacher gave isolated declarative recasts to grammatical or grammar-related incomplete sentence problems and repeated them twice in the episodes. The difference was the opportunity for learner repair; in Episode 1102 and 1106, which occurred during the group interaction, the original students had chances to repair. The error correction became explicit and isolated from the main discourse. In Test 1, Shoko's answers to items from these episodes were correct.

Table 1 Descriptions of the three episodes with different effects

Episode		Characteristics		Student reaction	Test 1
1102	Isolated declarative	Grammatical	Repeated	Student uptake	Both correct
1106	Isolated declarative	Grammatical	Repeated	Student uptake	Both correct
108	Isolated declarative	Incomplete (preposition)	Repeated	No opportunity	Both incorrect

However, in Episode 108, which occurred during teacher-fronted interaction, the teacher did not provide the original student with a chance to repair; instead the teacher continued the topic by extending her turn. This episode remained ambiguous with respect to its corrective function, and Shoko did not become aware of the corrective aspect of this episode. Her answers related to this item in Test 1 were wrong.

This finding suggests that the salience and explicitness of recast feedback could be attributed to the intention of the recast provider rather than the linguistic elements. The recasts in Doughty and Varela (1998), for example, were explicit, containing repetitiveness, phonological emphasis, and pauses for learner uptake, because the feedback was intentional.

Second, recasts occurring in communicatively meaningful interaction could have greater pedagogical usefulness. We found that recasts provided in group interaction were more likely perceived 'accurately' as correction, thus more likely to be effective than those provided in teacher-fronted interaction. As noted earlier, Shoko was more correct and confident with respect to group-related items in Test 1. This supports the positive findings from diadic interaction in experimental studies.

Further, the recasts were 'opportunities for learning' and what was learned from it depended on the learner. We found Shoko used recast feedback for other purposes independent from the error correction context. One example was using the recast feedback for understanding the meaning of 'right to vote'. Ignoring the grammatical correction the recast provided, Shoko focused on and learned something she autonomously identified in the episode: the meaning of 'right to vote'. In the case of 'right to vote', Shoko judged the relevant items correct in Test 2.

Finally, the 'repeated experience' and 'talking about experience' with which our research design provided Shoko, seemed to have influenced her learning. Test 2 results show this clearly. Shoko re-experienced the classroom interaction through watching videos before taking Test 2. Being an analytic learner, Shoko talked during the stimulated recall interviews about language; much of her interview protocol included a number of language-related episodes (Swain & Lapkin, 1998). The improvement from Test 1 to Test 2 suggests that repeated exposure to and experience of feedback as well as talking about the experience helped her learn English.

Conclusion

This case study explored the effect of recast feedback in a theme-based EFL classroom in relation to a learner's awareness. Although findings from this small case study focusing on one student cannot be generalised to other situations, our exploration made the complexity of recast feedback evident. It has been assumed that effects of feedback could be evaluated universally on the basis of linguistic elements of input and theory-driven contextual features (e.g. reactive model as opposed to pre-emptive model). Effectiveness of feedback, however, needs to be attributed to each discourse context, composed of the teacher and the learner, where the feedback is actually provided.

Shoko provided us with rich insightful data for understanding what she attended to and why, and how she learned the second language. She has shown that she is the agent in her own learning, choosing when to make use of the learning opportunities presented to her. She has also shown, as a methodological by-product in this case study, that verbalisation of her thought about using the language both in class and out of class helped her learn English. More studies of this kind, focusing on learners, and understanding them from *their* perspectives in different contexts are needed for our better understanding of recasts, feedback, and second language learning.

Each of these classroom studies has used a different approach to try to further understand how learners learn from classroom practice. Each study sheds some light on the complex nature of language learning within the social relations of the classroom, but each project can tell only part of the story. In the chapters which follow we will discuss other studies of language learning, both in and out of the classroom, that use different methodologies from the one described here, such as ethnography.

📖 Activity: Guided Reading

Reading 2:

Breen, M. P. (2001) 'The social context for language learning: a neglected situation?', in C. Candlin and N. Mercer (eds) *English Language Teaching in its Social Context: A Reader*. London, Routledge, pp. 122–134.

In Reading 2 Breen argues that no single research methodology is sufficient to answer all the questions.

1. Why does he criticize existing research into language classrooms?
2. Do you think the research by Nabei and Swain manages to do what Breen thinks most research does not do – that is, investigate both cognitive and social factors?

Introduction

I wish to explore the belief that the classroom will have certain effects upon language learning. The assumption resting within what I have to say is that relationships can be discovered between the social processes of the classroom group and the individual psychological process of second language development. Given the present state of our knowledge about the learning of foreign languages, this assumption is supported upon tenuous foundations. As most people at least begin to learn new languages in classrooms, the researcher can hardly fail to locate some variable of classroom life that will have a systematic effect upon language learning, or some variable of learning behaviour which has correlational potential with instructional treatment. The researcher may ask: "What are the *specific* contributions of the classroom to the process of language development?" The assumption being that we may be able to explain how classroom-based instruction influences and interacts with learning if we come to understand the special workings of the classroom context. The teacher's priorities – perhaps more urgent and direct – are to build upon those inherent features of the classroom situation which may facilitate the learning of a new language. The teacher's question may be: "In what ways might I exploit the social reality of the classroom as a *resource* for the teaching of language?"

This paper offers particular answers to both the researcher's and the teacher's questions. It begins with an examination of the approaches of current research towards the language class. I offer a particular evaluation of recent developments in investigations devoted to second language acquisition and to language learning in the classroom situation. This evaluation, though necessarily brief, has three purposes. First, to identify the possible contributions of the language classroom which are perceived and revealed by current research. Second, to identify what seem to be significant contributions of the classroom which current research appears to neglect. And third, to deduce certain implications for future research and for language teaching.

The researcher and the teacher are confronted by a crucial common problem: how to relate social activity, to psychological change and how to relate psychological processing to the social dynamics of a group. The researcher must explain these relationships if he is to understand adequately language learning as it is experienced by most people – in a gathering made up of other learners and a teacher. The teacher is a direct participant in this social event with the aim of influencing psychological development. The teacher is obliged continually to integrate the learning experiences of individuals with the collective and communal activities of a group of which, unlike the researcher, he is not an outsider. The researcher enters the classroom when a genuine sociocognitive experiment is already well under way. In evaluating the findings of research, because of abstraction from the daily life of the class, we need to discover and make clear for ourselves the particular *perceptions* of a classroom which we, as researchers, hold either before we enter it or subsequent to the collection of our data. It is a truism of social anthropology that no human social institutions or relationships can be adequately understood unless account is taken of the expectations, values, and beliefs that they engage. This is no less true of the institution of research. The definition of the classroom situation that we hold will influence how we perceive the classroom group and how we might act within it, and this is as unavoidable for the researcher as it is for a teacher or a learner. One of the paradoxes of research is to challenge taken-for-granted beliefs whilst, at the same time, clinging to beliefs which sustain the research endeavour. Belief allows the researcher (and many teachers and learners) to take for granted the capacity of a classroom to metamorphose instructional inputs into learning outcomes. Is there psychological proof for this relationship between teaching and learning, or is it a belief sustained primarily by the social purpose *that we invest* in a gathering of teacher and taught?

Can we detect particular definitions of the classroom situation within current language learning research? What metaphors for a classroom are available to us as researchers at present? I wish to explore two metaphors for the classroom that emerge from two recent and influential research traditions. I am conscious that there may be as many metaphors for the classroom as there are researchers in language learning. But I have to be brief and I am encouraged to generalise here by the tendency of researchers to seek security around particular dominant paradigms or ways of seeing. One prevailing metaphor is the classroom as experimental laboratory, and another, more recently emergent, is the classroom as discourse. I will briefly explore both.

The classroom as experimental laboratory

We are encouraged to regard the classroom as experimental laboratory by the area of theory and research known as Second Language Acquisition (SLA). Its tradition can be traced back to studies in first language acquisition, through investigation of the natural order of acquisition of certain grammatical morphemes, through the comprehensive theories of Krashen, and up to the recent flowering in the identification of learner strategies from retrospective accounts offered by individual learners – either verbally or within learning diaries. The primary function of the language classroom as implied or sometimes directly recommended by SLA research is that the learner, by being placed in a classroom, can be exposed to a certain kind of linguistic input which may be shown to correlate with certain desirable learning outcomes. Here, the value and purpose of the classroom is its potential to provide linguistic data that are finely tuned for the efficient processing of new knowledge; classrooms can wash learners with optimal input. Researchers' more recent inferences from learners' accounts of their own strategies encourage us to deduce further that the classroom is a place in which we might reinforce good language-learning strategies so that the input becomes unavoidably optimal. As the mainstream of SLA research rests on the assumption that the comprehension. of input is the catalyst of language development, it implies a role for the teacher that is delimited yet complex. In essence, either the teacher must facilitate comprehension through the provision of linguistic input sensitive to individual learner inclinations, or the teacher should endeavour to shape individual learning behaviours so that each learner may attain a repertoire of efficient processing strategies. The SLA metaphor for the classroom implies teacher as surrogate experimental psychologist and learners as subject to particular input treatments or behavioural reinforcement.

However, this view of the language classroom leaves us with a number of unresolved problems that warrant more attention if we seek to understand the relationship between a language class and language learning. First, the interesting variables of linguistic input and the strategic behaviour of learners *are not special to classrooms*. They were not uncovered as prevailing features of classroom life at all. The second and perhaps more significant problem is that two crucial intervening variables seem to have been bypassed by SLA research. Both of these variables are centrally related to the processing of input. Both will determine what a learner might actually *intake*. SLA research which emphasises linguistic input (provided by instruction or exposure) as the independent variable and some later learner output (in a test or in spontaneous speech) as the dependent variable leaps blindly over any active cognition on the part of the learner. With its heavy reliance on linguistic performance criteria for psychological change there is a resultant superficiality in its attention to learners' internal perceptual processes. The research takes for granted what the *learner* may define as optimal for him. More fundamentally, it does not address the question of *how* a learner selectively perceives parts of linguistic data as meaningful and worth acting upon in the first place. Therefore, the intervening variable of what the learner actually does to input or with input is neglected. Given the importance attached to comprehension by SLA research it seems paradoxical that the active reinterpretation and reconstruction of any input by the learner is not accounted for. The search for correlations between, for example, the frequency of a grammatical form in input and the frequent occurrence of that form in some later learner performance seems motivated by a rather narrow view of human learning. The research leads us to a causal conditioning as opposed to a cognitive and interactive explanation of language development. We are left unsure *how and why* learners do what they do in order to intake selectively.

On the face of it, learning strategy research seems to offer some help here. However, these investigations primarily confirm that learners are unpredictable, inconsistent, and sometimes seemingly inefficient processors. Thus, the same learning outcome can be achieved by different strategies while different learning outcomes can be achieved by the same strategy. Investigations into learner strategies have not yet helped us to understand how or why it is that one thing can be interpreted or learned by any two learners with seemingly different profiles of strategies. Until we understand these things, the capacity of instruction to encourage or shape desirable or efficient strategic behaviour of learners remains unfounded. This problem emerging from the data we derive from learners concerning their strategies leads to the second crucial intervening variable which seems to be neglected in SLA research. Learners certainly are strategic in how they go about learning, but if we ask them what they think they do, or if they keep a diary of what they do, such retrospections, inevitably *post hoc* rationalisations, will exhibit a coherence that bears only metaphorical resemblance to the actual moment of learning. Something intervenes between a learner's introspections to a researcher or to a diary reader, just as something intervenes between input to a learner and between what a learner has intaken and some later test performance. I suggest that one thing which crucially intervenes is the learner's definition of situation: the definition of being an informant to someone investigating strategies, the definition of being a language learner in a classroom, and the definition of doing a test. If we hope to explain fully the relationship between classroom input and learning outcomes, or to explain possible relationships between strategic behaviour and language learning, then we need to locate these relationships *socially*. How and why learners do what they do will be strongly influenced by their situation, who they are with, and by their perceptions of both.

Given that we wish to understand how the external social situation of a classroom relates to the internal psychological states of the learner, the metaphor of the classroom as provider of optimal input or reinforcer of good strategies is inadequate. It *reduces* the act or experience of learning a language to linguistic or behavioural conditioning somehow independent of the learner's social reality. Not only is SLA research currently offering us a delimited account of language learning, reducing active cognition to passive internalisation and reducing language to very specific grammatical performance, the mainstream of SLA research is also asocial. It neglects the social significance of even those variables which the investigators regard as central. The priority given to linguistic and mentalistic variables in terms of the efficient processing of knowledge as input leads inevitably to a partial account of the language learning process. The social context of learning and the social forces within it will always shape what is made available to be learned *and* the interaction of individual mind with external linguistic or communicative knowledge. Even Wundt, the first experimental psychologist, believed that he could not study higher mental processes such as reasoning, belief, thought, and language in a *laboratory* precisely because such processes were rooted within authentic social activity. A more recent research tradition – an offspring of work in SLA – does address intervening social variables. This tradition provides my second metaphor.

The classroom as discourse

Recent classroom-based or classroom-oriented research explicitly seeks to describe what actually happens in a rather special social situation. This research relies upon methods of conversational and sociolinguistic data collection and analysis, thereby seeking to offer a richer and less prescriptive account of classroom language learning than earlier investigations of the comparative effects of different teaching method-ologies. Classroom-oriented research focuses primarily upon the discourse of classroom communication. It sees teacher and learners as active participants in the generation of the discourse of lessons. Here, the researcher explores the classroom as a text which reveals such phenomena as variable participation by learners, various error treatments by teachers, and specific features of classroom talk such as teacher evaluation, teacher–learner negotiation, and prevalent instructional speech acts including display questions, formulation or explanation, and message adjustment. Although much of this research seems to avoid being intentionally explanatory in terms of the possible effects of classroom discourse upon language learning, some investigators seek to correlate selected features of classroom talk with certain learning behaviours or learned outcomes. Classroom-oriented research rests on the assumption that the discourse of a language class will reveal what is special and important about that language learning situation. It intends no practical implications for the teacher, although some of the more overtly correlational studies may encourage the teacher to assume that he must endeavour to orchestrate his own and the learners' contributions to the discourse according to conversational moves or speech acts which exemplify "good" instruction and "good" learner participation.

Clearly, this focus upon the actual discourse of classroom communication provides a valid location if we wish to begin to understand the experience of learning a language in a classroom. However, even with such an ecologically valid point of departure, current classroom-oriented research leaves us with two important areas of uncertainty. We have to question the extent to which the surface text of classroom discourse can adequately reveal the underlying social psychological forces which generate it (the expectations, beliefs and attitudes of the participants) and also reveal the sociocognitive effects it may have (the specific interpretations and learning it provokes). This central issue leads us back into the long-established debate on the possible relationships between communicating and learning, between language and cognition. A number of the correlational studies within classroom-oriented research avoid the complexities of this debate by appearing to assume that certain phenomena in classroom discourse *cause* learning to occur. Any correlation between observable features of discourse and testable learning outcomes – a teacher's formulation of a rule, for example, and a learner's later use or refor-mulation of that rule – does not explain how or why a learner actually achieved such things. This dependency on the superficial features of classroom talk can force us to deduce that if other learners in the class failed to use the rule correctly or were unable to reformulate it then the teacher's original formulation was inadequate. But what of the internal dimensions of classroom communication: the learners' variable perception, reinterpretation, and accommodation of whatever may be provided through classroom discourse? In these matters, classroom-oriented research seems to share a psychological naivety with SLA research.

The second area of uncertainty is perhaps more fundamental. Most current classroom-oriented research paradoxically reduces the external dimensions of classroom communication, the actual social event, to observable features of the talk between teacher and learners. Sixty years ago, Edward Sapir pointed out that we cannot use observable data alone from social events even if we merely aim to describe them adequately. Nor can we interpret the observable data through our eyes only if we ever seek to explain what those data actually *mean*. Even Del Hymes, who was foremost in proposing the ethnography of speaking which now underlies much sociolinguistic research, also insisted that if we wish adequately to explain any speech event we need to discover its existential and experiential significance for those taking part. These proposals imply that the meanings and values of classroom discourse reside behind and beneath what is said and unsaid. A researcher's interpretation of the "text" of classroom discourse has to be derived through the participants' interpretations of that discourse. Is the teacher's treatment of an error taken as error treatment by a learner? Is a learner's request for information – even if responded to as such by the teacher – actually a piece of time-wasting or even expressing something else entirely? Is superficial negotiation of meaning or a learner's generation of further input evidence of the wish to learn more?

To begin to understand language learning experience in a classroom the researcher must discover what teacher and taught themselves perceive as inherent within the discourse of lessons. More importantly, recent classroom research clearly shows the researcher as someone who *invests* into his text of classroom discourse certain patternedness or meaningfulness. Classroom communication, like any text, realizes and carries meaning potential. Because of this, if we wish to discover what the teaching and learning of a language in a classroom is for the people undertaking

it, we need to know what orderliness and sense *they invest* in the overt communication of the class. Put simply, the discourse of the classroom does not itself reveal
what the teacher and the learners experience from that discourse. Such experience
is two-dimensional: individual-subjective experience and collective-intersubjective
experience. The subjective experience of teacher and learners in a classroom is
woven with personal purposes, attitudes, and preferred ways of doing things.
The intersubjective experience derives from and maintains teacher and learner
shared definitions, conventions, and procedures which enable a working together
in a crowd. Of course, the discourse of a classroom may provide a window onto
the surface expression of the intersubjective experience and even onto momentary
expressions of subjective experiences, for these two dimensions of experience must
interrelate and influence one another. However, classroom discourse alone allows
us a partial view from which we are obliged to describe others' experiences as if
"through a glass darkly."

. . .

It appears that the two metaphors for the classroom which we have available to
us at present offer definitions of the classroom situation which seem to neglect
the social reality of language learning *as it is experienced and created* by teachers and
learners. Both metaphors unfortunately constrain our understanding of language
learning because each takes for granted crucial intervening psychological and
social variables which are the fulcra upon which language learning is balanced. The
reconstructive cognition of learners and the social and psychological forces which
permeate the processes of teaching and learning must reside within any explanation
concerning how and why people do what they do when they work together on a
new language. More seriously, perhaps, both contemporary metaphors implicitly
reduce human action and interaction to classical conditioning, wherein learners
though superficially participating are essentially passive respondents to observable
linguistic and discoursal stimuli. It therefore appears necessary that research has still
to adopt a definition of the classroom which will encompass *both cognitive and social
variables* so that their mutual influence can be better understood. More precisely,
we need a metaphor for the classroom through which teacher and learners can be
viewed as thinking social actors and not reduced to generators of input-output
nor analyzed as dualities of either conceptual or social beings. Perhaps the metaphor
we require can provide a basis for the synthesis of SLA and classroom-oriented
research endeavours whilst necessarily being more comprehensive than both. These
deductions lead me to propose a third metaphor for the classroom in the hope that
it might further facilitate our understanding of classroom language learning. One of
the characteristics of my third metaphor is that it is likely to be more *experientially*
familiar to most language teachers and learners than it may be to some researchers.

The classroom as coral gardens

A proposal that the classroom situation could be perceived as coral gardens may be initially reacted to as rather odd. The metaphor derives from Malinowski's classical studies of Trobriand island cultures, in particular those investigations he described in *Coral Gardens and Their Magic*. I offer the metaphor because it entails three requirements for research devoted to classroom language learning. First, in order to understand the process of learning within a human group, our investigations are necessarily an anthropological endeavour. Second, the researcher should approach the classroom with a kind of anthropological humility. We should explore classroom life initially as if we knew nothing about it. And, third, it is more important to discover what people invest in a social situation than it is to rely on what might be observed as inherent in that social situation. Just as gardens of coral were granted magical realities by the Trobriand islanders, a language class – outwardly a gathering of people with an assumed common purpose – is an arena of subjective and inter-subjective realities which are worked out, changed, and maintained. *And these realities are not trivial background to the tasks of teaching and learning a language*. They locate and define the new language itself as if it never existed before, and they continually specify and mould the activities of teaching and learning. In essence, the metaphor of classroom as coral gardens insists that we perceive the language class as a genuine culture and worth investigating as such.

If we can adopt this definition of the classroom situation, then research may get closer to the daily lives of teachers and learners. We can approach the raison d'être of a language class – the working upon and rediscovering of language knowl-edge – as involving sociocognitive construction and reinterpretation. A particular culture, by definition, entails particular relationships between social activities and psychological processes and changes. SLA research asserts comprehension as central, whilst the classroom as culture locates comprehension within the intersubjective construction of meaningfulness and the subjective reinterpretation of whatever may be rendered comprehensible. In other words, input is never inherently optimal, for any new knowledge is socio-cognitively rendered familiar or unfamiliar by those who participate in its exploration. The culture of the class *generates knowledges* and a focus upon any internalised linguistic outcomes will tell us little about classroom language learning in action. Classroom-oriented research explores the discourse of lessons, whilst the classroom as culture extends across islands of intersubjective meaning and depths of subjective intentions and interpretations which only rarely touch the surface of talk and which the discourse itself often deliberately hides. The discourse of lessons will mainly *symbolise* what participants contribute to those lessons and it will not signify what they actually invest in them or derive from them.

It is, of course, incumbent upon me to justify my own belief in the classroom as genuine culture. In order to meet the charge that such a metaphor may be too idealised or abstract, I need to identify some of the essential features of the culture of the language classroom. I will briefly describe eight essential features:

The culture of the classroom is interactive

The language class involves all its participants in verbal and non-verbal interaction of certain kinds. This interaction exists on a continuum from ritualised, predictable, phatic communication to dynamic, unpredictable, diversely interpreted communication. Of course, human interaction will be relatively located on this kind of continuum in all social situations. One special characteristic of classroom interaction, however, is that it is motivated by the assumption that people can learn together in a group. This means that a high premium is placed upon consensus whilst misunderstandings, alternative interpretations, and negotiable meaning will paradoxically be the norm, and from which participants will seek to make their own sense and upon which participants will impose their own purposes. This is not to say that the observable interaction will not be patterned or constrained, but that it is very likely to be patterned differently in the interpretations invested in it by each person in the class. Therefore the researcher needs to be wary of assuming that the patterns of interaction which we perceive as significant have the same salience for both teacher and taught. A special characteristic of the language class is that interaction is further motivated by the assumption that people can objectify a language and talk about it and analyse it in ways they may not naturally do if left alone. The language class implies metalinguistic interaction. However, it is often further assumed that the language class can provide opportunities for genuine interaction through the new language code. A language class entails interaction about language and interaction through *languages* in continual juxtaposition.

All these and other characteristics of the interactive process of the language class may or may not be efficient or optimal for language learning. However, all represent the *inherent authenticity* of the interaction within a language class given the external constraints of space, time, participation, etc., which typify any classroom devoted to any subject matter. A significant paradox for the language teacher – a paradox of which teachers are well aware – is that the established interaction which is evolved and maintained by the culture of the classroom group often conflicts with efforts towards communication through the new language. Communication in the new language requires the temporary suspension of those cultural conventions governing the everyday interaction of the particular classroom group. It requires communication which is, in fact, *inauthentic* to the interactive context in which it has to occur. This implies that one of the conventions assumed to be honoured by participants in the culture of a language class is the willingness and capacity to suspend disbelief, to participate in simulated communication *within* classroom-specific interaction.

The culture of the classroom is differentiated

Although the language class may be one social situation, it is a different social *context* for all those who participate within it. The culture of the classroom is an amalgam and permutation of different social realities. This means that the content of lessons (the language being taught) and the procedures of teaching and learning (the things being done) are both continually interpreted differently as the life of that language class unfolds. The classroom is the meeting point of various subjective views of language, diverse learning purposes, and different preferences concerning how learning should be done. Such differentiation brings with it potential for disagreement, frustrated expectations, and conflict. The culture of the classroom does not erase these differences; it contains them. A major challenge for teacher and learners is the maintenance of a fine balance between conflicting internal social realities (a kind of subjective anarchy!) and an external reality which has to be *continually negotiated*. The outside observer has access to the compromise which results, but we would be naive to deduce that such a compromise represents what is actually intended or perceived as the social reality for any one person in the class.

The culture of the classroom is collective

The culture of the classroom represents a tension between the internal world of the individual and the social world of the group, a recurrent juxtaposition of personal learning experiences and communal teaching-learning activities and conventions. The culture of the class has a psychological reality, a mind of its own, which emerges from this juxtaposition. The psyche of the group – the group's values, meanings, and volitions – is a distinct entity other than the sum of the individual psychological orientations of teacher and learners. Socially, the sometimes ritualised and sometimes overtly dynamic behaviour of the group will both contain and influence the behaviour of the individual just as the overt contributions of a teacher or a learner will fit, or divert the workings of the class. But this social framework builds upon and constructs a particular world which has to be accommodated as a point of departure for psychological change. A teacher and a learner have to discover *that* definition of situation which seems to maintain the group and its activities – *that* definition of situation which will be relatively distinct from their personal definitions. This involves all members of the group in empathising with the roles and views of others and continually checking such external frames of reference. The individual has to adapt his learning process to the social-psychological resources of the group. So also the group's psychic and social process will unfold from the individual contributions of a learner. This interplay between individual and collective consciousness (and the values, beliefs, and attitudes it generates) implies that the researcher should be wary of crediting the classroom with powers separable from what individual learners actually *make* classrooms do for them, and similarly wary of crediting individual learners with powers separable from what the classroom group provides. An individual learner in a classroom is engaged in both an individual learning process *and* a group teaching-learning process. Therefore individual psychological change will continually relate to group psychological forces. The researcher is obliged to discover these two worlds because they are distinctive. To *infer* individual learning process from classroom process or vice versa will lead to a partial understanding of classroom language learning. We need to explore both and how they relate one to the other.

The culture of the classroom is highly normative

Our membership in any culture implies that our behaviour will be evaluated against certain norms and conventions – membership entails *showing* we belong. However, in all our lives, classrooms are very special in this regard. Schools and classrooms are among the main agencies for secondary socialisation and, as the first public institution most of us enter during our lives, our views of classrooms will be significantly coloured by this initial experience. More importantly, our personal identities as learners within a group derive much from such experience. This is due to the fact that our public learning selves have been moulded by a continual and explicit evaluation of *our worth as learners*. When a language learner enters a classroom, he anticipates that the evaluation of him as a learner is going to be a crucial part of that experience. This implies that the search for external criteria for success in coping with language learning and, less optimistically perhaps, the day-to-day search for ways of reducing the potential threat of negative judgements of one's capabilities will impinge upon whatever internal criteria a learner may evolve regarding his own learning progress. Learners in a class will obviously vary with regard to their relative dependence upon external and internal criteria. However, one of the prevalent features of the culture of the classroom is the establishment of overt and covert criteria against which its members are continually judged. In other words, the culture of the classroom *reifies* the persons who participate within it into "good" learners and "bad" learners, "good" teachers and "bad" teachers, "beginners," "advanced," "high" participators and "low" participators, etc., etc. Put bluntly, the language class is a highly normative and evaluative environment which engages teacher and taught in continual judgement of each other, less as persons, but as members who are supposed to learn and as the member who is supposed to teach. This highly normative characteristic of classroom life implies for the researcher that we need to discover the overt and covert group criteria (*and* members' individual interpretations of these criteria) against which learning behaviour and progress are judged. To infer, for example, that a teacher's error corrections are consistently based upon objective linguistic criteria or are otherwise apparently random would lead to a superficial analysis of phenomena which, though opaque, are deeply significant for a teacher and learners in the particular classroom.

The culture of the classroom is asymmetrical

Because teachers are expected to know what learners are expected not to know, certain social and psychological consequences inevitably obtain for the human relationships in the class. The culture of the classroom insists upon asymmetrical relationships. The duties and rights of teacher and taught are different. More significantly, both teacher and taught may be *equally reluctant* to upset the asymmetry of roles and identities to which these duties and rights are assigned. In most societies – perhaps all, despite some relative variation – an egalitarian relationship between teacher and taught is a contradiction of what a classroom should be. Teachers and learners are very familiar with the experience of gradually establishing the precise degree of asymmetry which enables them to maintain a relatively harmonious working group. As teachers, we are also familiar with a class which erodes what they perceive as being too democratic or too authoritarian an approach on our part, even though we ourselves may perceive our teaching style as consistently something else entirely! Here is a paradox. Learners *give* a teacher the right to adopt a role and identity of teacher. And a teacher has to *earn* particular rights and duties in the eyes of the learning group. However, the history of the tribe marches behind the teacher, and a teacher *through* the unfolding culture of the particular classroom group will similarly allocate rights and duties to learners. Indeed, one of the rights and duties of a teacher is to do precisely that! However, asymmetrical relationships do not only exist between teacher and taught. Sub-groupings which are asymmetrical with the dominant classroom culture also emerge and prosper, such as anti-academic peer groupings or certain learners who identify themselves as more successful or less successful and even groups who share a common identity (such as friendship groups) outside the classroom. Thus, not only is the culture of the classroom individually differentiated yet collective, it is also made up of sub-groups which develop for themselves mainly covert, though sometimes overtly expressed, roles and identities which are potentially asymmetrical with both the dominant culture and with other sub-groupings in the class.

Asymmetry of roles and identities, and of the rights and duties they bear, derives from and further generates conceptual and affective dissonances. Asymmetrical relationships very often entail disagreement in beliefs, in attitudes, and in values held. The collective nature of the classroom culture and the negotiated compromises which permeate the teaching-learning process often hide within themselves – sometimes with difficulty and often only for a time – different views of what should be happening in a class and what should not. This suggests that, although the nature of interpersonal and intergroup relationships within the language classroom may be complex and changing, the researcher needs to uncover what these are if we wish to describe what happens in the class and further interpret this as it is experienced by those within the class. As researchers in the past, we have tended to be teacher-centred in our assuming that the major asymmetry in role and identity, and the likely location of dissonance in perceptions and effects, resides between the teacher and the rest. We have also perhaps underestimated the possible effects – both negative and positive – of asymmetry and dissonance within the classroom upon the language learning process.

The culture of the classroom is inherently conservative

Perhaps one of the best ways of revealing the established culture of the classroom group is to try to introduce an innovation which the majority neither expects nor defines as appropriate. Most teachers have had direct experience of the effort to be radical in their approach with a class (be it through different material, tasks, or procedure, etc.) and have suffered the experience of at least initial rejection. A genuine culture is one in which its members seek security and relative harmony in a self-satisfactory milieu. As such things take time to develop, anything which the group perceives as change will also take time to be absorbed or it will be resisted as deviant. (This does not mean that harmony will necessarily reign in the classroom, for even apparent anarchy – as long as it is the preferred ethos of that group – may be quite consistent with a definition of classroom life for some seemingly unsocialised collection of learners!). In essence, a classroom group seeks a particular social and emotional equilibrium just as soon as it can – even one which may seem to be antithetical to learning. It will subsequently resist any threat to the newly established order. The individual learner risks ostracisation from the group if he does not – overtly at least – conform, and the teacher risks rebellion in various forms if he does not honour the conventions expected by the collective definition of what a language teacher should be. Although this conservative spirit has its origins in the prior educational experiences of the learners, each new classroom group reinvents "the rules of the game" in ways which both reflect and form the classroom-culture assumptions of the particular participants who are suddenly sharing each others' company. It has to be said, of course, that a teacher may participate in this conservatism and, indeed, work *through* it in order to help develop group harmony, security and efficient ways of working. And teachers are certainly familiar with the dilemma of wishing to innovate whilst being cautious of disruption. This means that the very presence of a researcher, or even the awareness within the group that they are the focus of apparently objective evaluation and study will mobilise change. Our personal experience of having someone visit our home for the first time and then looking at it with them, as if seeing it through their eyes, can remind us of the effect of intrusion. In a sense, the classroom changes in the eyes of those within it and, therefore, *will* change in certain ways. This is, of course, the truism of observer effect. But there is also the observer's paradox in that the classroom we now see will be in a state of disequilibrium: it will not be the same classroom as yesterday and we will be investigating a classroom group which is newly adapting in a number of subtle ways. This phenomenon can be either bad news or good news for the researcher. It will render short-term, one-shot investigations into classroom language learning largely invalid and unreliable. If, on the other hand, we approach studies of classroom language learning on a longitudinal basis, then we may be able to explore the process of re-establishment of social and emotional equilibrium which our initial arrival challenged. In other words, we may uncover more precisely the "rules of the game" which represent the self-maintaining culture of that particular working group.

The culture of the classroom is jointly constructed

Whilst we may accept the truism that all knowledge is socially constructed – most especially if we are working with the knowledge of a language and how it is used between people – we need to consider how classrooms *re-construct* knowledge. In a language class, the classroom group together not only freshly evolves the new language (the content of lessons), but together also jointly constructs the lessons (the social procedures of teaching and learning). Whether or not the teacher plans a lesson in advance, the actual working out of that lesson in the class demands joint endeavour. The lesson-in-process is most often different from that which either the teacher or the learners anticipated before the lesson began. The social dynamic of the group insists that lessons evolve, through explicit or implicit negotiation. In whatever ways the lesson may be perceived by those who participate in it, the route it takes will be drawn by the joint contributions of most, if not all, of the members of the class. Teachers and learners are well aware that lessons are rarely straightforward journeys but are punctuated by hesitant starts, diversions, momentary losses of momentum, interesting side tracks, and unexpected breakdowns. That it may be better to plan classroom learning in advance has little to do with this entirely normal and creative evolution of lessons.

Several important implications for the researcher result from the fact that the content and process of language classes are jointly constructed. First, any teacher-centred (or researcher-centred) perspective on lessons is partial. Second, the researcher's background knowledge of the actual language being worked upon in a class can be a serious handicap because it potentially blinds us to the process of re-invention of that language which teacher and taught engage in together. (This implication warns us against relying on external linguistic criteria alone in assessing the nature of comprehensible input, for example.) The problem reminds us of a similar gap between the teacher's definition of the new language and the different learners' definitions. There are likely to be as many versions of the new language, and changing versions of it, as there are people in the room. Third, the researcher has to be continually wary of being dazzled by what *seems* salient in classroom life. For example, even the most passive or non-contributory learner in a class can be a poltergeist on the proceedings. Silence, encouraged or not, is a characteristic part of the culture of the classroom and it has great significance. Silence or withdrawal can change a lesson just as powerfully as their opposites, and not just for the person who withdraws, but also for all the others who sense it. The fourth implication of the joint construction of the content and process of a language class is particularly significant for researchers who wish to examine the effects of classroom language learning. The fact that lessons-in-process are communal endeavours means that *any learning outcome*, for any member of the class, has been socially processed. The actual nature of individual achievements has been communally moulded. The culture of the classroom inevitably mediates between a new language and a learner in class. The culture of a particular class will shape what is made available for learning, will work upon what is made available in particular ways, will evolve its own criteria for progress and achievement, and will attain specific and various objectives. (It is worth emphasising here that linguistic input is only a part of the first of these classroom-based phenomena.) What someone learns in a language class will be a dynamic synthesis of individual *and* collective experience. Individual definitions of the new language, of what is to be attended to as worth learning, of how to learn, and personal definitions of progress will all *interact with* the particular classroom culture's definitions of each of these things. If strictly individualised or autonomous language learning is desirable or even possible then the classroom is necessarily antithetical towards it. The language I learn in a classroom is a communal product derived through a jointly constructed process.

The culture of the classroom is immediately significant

What is overtly done in a classroom and what can be described by an observer are *epiphenomena*; they are reductions of classroom reality. How things are done and why things are done have particular psychological significance for the individual and for the group. The particular culture of a language class will socially act in certain ways, but these actions are extensions or manifestations of the psychology of the group, its collective consciousness and subconscious. Individual perceptions and definitions will, of course, feed into and evolve from those of the group. However, the socio-cognitive world of the class – its culture – will be a world other than the sum of the individual worlds within it. What is *significant* for learners (and a teacher) in a classroom is not only their individual thinking and behaviour nor, for instance, a longer-term mastery of a syllabus, but the day-to-day interpersonal rationalisation of what is to be done, why, and how. The immediate significance of the experience of classroom language learning resides in how individual priorities (teacher and learner definitions of what, why, and how) can be given social space here and now. It is precisely this interplay between the individual, the individual as group member, and the group which represents and generates the social and psychological *nexus* which I have proposed as the culture of the language classroom. Most often the flow of classroom life is actually under the surface. What is observable is the rim of a socio-cognitive coral reef! Classroom life *seems* to require that many learners spend surprising amounts of time doing little, whilst a teacher spends equally surprising amounts of time trying to do too much. As researchers we can describe such overt peculiarities, but we also need to explain them. We have to ask whether or not such phenomena are true, and we must doubt the integrity of the observable. If we do, then we are led towards discovering what is, in fact, immediately significant for the group of people we started to observe. The search for the significance which a person, learner or teacher, invests in moments of classroom life (and for the significance granted to these moments by the classroom culture) is neither trivial nor avoidable, though it may be complex and subtle. We will never understand classroom language learning unless we explore its lesson-by-lesson significance for those who undertake it.

Discussion

1. In Reading 2 Michael Breen argues that we should study classroom learning as an anthropologist studies a new culture. He puts forward eight essential categories of such a classroom culture: interactive, differentiated, collective, normative, asymmetrical, conservative, jointly constructed, and immediately significant (pp. 129–134).

Can you provide any illustrations of events from your teaching experience or learners you have encountered who would support or counter any of these categories?

2. The research by Nabei and Swain in Reading 1 took place in a monolingual foreign language classroom, and aimed to capture some of the learning process of one particular learner.

What do the insights into this particular learner's language acquisition process in a particular learning situation tell us about the language learning process in general?

3. In Reading 2 after the extract included here, Breen goes on to suggest that teachers and learners together should investigate the language learning process as part of language learning in the classroom. Nabei and Swain found that Shoko improved her knowledge of English through her participation in the research.

Do you think explicit discussion and exploration of the language-learning process in the classroom is a good idea for ESOL contexts?

Research

Tape-record one class you are teaching, or are involved in (as long as the students agree).

As you play the tape back listen for all the episodes of error correction (you could transcribe these if you have time).

The following questions may help you analyse these episodes and reflect on their role in the language classroom:

*   Who initiated each correction: teacher or fellow students?
*   What kind of correction is it? (See the list of types on p. 13.)
*   What is the student's response?

Additional reading

Barton, D. and Pitt, K. (2003) 'Adult ESOL pedagogy: a review of research, an annotated bibliography and recommendations for further research'. National Research and Development Centre Research Review (downloadable from the NRDC website).

Chapter 2

The good language learner
Changing definitions?

Introduction

In this chapter we turn from language-learning processes that are thought to be general to all learners to studies that are concerned with identifying differences between the ways individuals learn an additional language. Researchers have tried to find out why some learners seem to learn faster and become more proficient in a language than others. Over the years research on the 'good language learner' has focused on factors such as age, aptitude, personality, motivation, attitude and learning strategies (for an overview of these, see Larsen-Freeman, 2001).

In many of these studies hypotheses are made about a particular characteristic of learners; tests or questionnaires are designed to measure the factor; various groups of learners are asked to undertake these tests and the results are analysed. Some studies have asked learners to keep diaries in order to explore emotions and learning styles. Other studies have used a variety of methods, to try to understand the strategies used by learners during specific language-learning tasks. An example of one of these methods is the think-aloud protocol in which learners describe their thoughts while carrying out a specific language task. This method, and others which investigate learner strategies, is explained and evaluated by Anna Chamot in Reading 2 of this chapter.

Most of this research has focused on the characteristics of individuals who are learning the language. The particular social relations within which individuals learn have been alluded to but not actively explored. This emphasis on the internal processes and states of learners has been criticized. In addition, much of this research has been concerned with foreign language learners rather than those learning the dominant language of the country they are living in as migrants, refugees or asylum seekers. Questions about the impact of class, gender and ethnicity on individual language learning were not part of this earlier research, but more recent research has explored these factors and some of this research is discussed in Reading 1 of this chapter.

In this chapter we consider some of the studies of individual differences in additional language learning that are relevant to the situations of ESOL learners in the UK. These will be used to reflect on the current debates over cognitive and social research perspectives. We also consider two factors which can affect the language learning of ESOL learners that have not usually been included in discussions of individual variations. The first of these is the effect of traumatic experiences on language learning. There is always the possibility that one or more of the learners in an ESOL class is suffering from trauma because of his or her experiences as a refugee or asylum seeker. The second factor is the condition called dyslexia. The increasing emphasis on the written language within education and the workplace has brought to the fore a set of problems experienced by some readers and writers of the English language. As more knowledge is being gathered about these problems among speakers of English as a first language, so questions are being asked about how they may affect ESOL learners.

The question of motivation

Many studies have explored the relationships between learners' attitudes towards the target language, their motivation to learn and learning performance. One such study of attitude and motivation was conducted with adult ESOL learners in the UK in 1989 (Khanna *et al.*, 1998). The researchers hypothesized that those learners who held positive attitudes towards both the English language and British people would have higher levels of proficiency in English. They drew up a list of words representing stereotypical attributes that could describe the English language (sweet, scientific, civilized, useful, easy) and stereotypical traits that could apply to British people or their own linguistic communities (hardworking, helpful, confident, efficient, successful, friendly, honest, dependable, educated). Participants indicated which attributes they considered were applicable to the English language, British people and their own community.

The researchers explored motivation by designing a set of ten statements based on the notion of motivation being either integrative or instrumental. An example of a statement illustrating the integrative outlook was 'You are learning English to think and behave as the English do'. An example of a statement illustrating the instrumental outlook was 'You are learning English to get a good job'. In previous studies of motivation it had been argued that those who had a friendly attitude and a desire to identify with the group whose language was being learned (an integrative outlook) would be more successful language learners.

The keywords and statements formed part of a questionnaire which was translated into several languages and given to 108 adult ESOL learners in Edinburgh, York, Leeds, Bradford, Walsall, London and Cardiff. Most of the informants were in the age group of 15 to 45 and two-thirds were female. The largest groups were from India, Pakistan and Bangladesh, and twenty-four were from China, Hong Kong, Korea and other Asian countries. Seventy-one had been in Britain for less than ten years. The researchers also sought information about the language proficiency of those participating in the study by asking their teachers to grade the informants' levels of speaking, listening, reading and writing.

As may be predicted, the informants did not express wholly positive attitudes, nor did they indicate an integrative outlook overall. A high percentage rated the

English language as 'useful', but responses to 'sweet', 'scientific' and 'easy' were only moderately positive. Over half of them did not think that the English language was at all 'civilized'. With regard to the stereotypical traits, the informants were mostly positive about those which have an achievement orientation. They regarded the British people as 'successful', 'educated', 'efficient' and 'confident', but they ranked their own community higher on 'hardworking' and 'friendly'. They did not rank either the British people or their own community highly as 'honest' or 'dependable'. Adding to these pragmatic attitudes, they selected instrumental rather than integrative reasons for learning English. When the individual question-naire responses were compared to their language proficiency, as rated by their teachers, no significant relationships were found between attitude, motivation and language learning.

However, the researchers not only collected information on psychological perspectives; they also asked, in the questionnaire, for information about the informants' language use in different domains of their lives, their exposure to English, their family's use of English and how they rated their own level of English proficiency. After analysis, significant correlations were found between the teachers' gradings, the informants' use of English at work and their self-rating of English ability. On the basis of these findings the researchers argued that a learner who uses English at work and has a positive image of her own capabilities is likely to be a successful language learner. The frequency of use of English in the home and exposure to it were also related to language levels.

📖 Activity: Guided Reading

Reading 1:

Norton, B. and Toohey, K. (2001) 'Changing perspectives on good language learners', *TESOL Quarterly* 35(2): 307–310, 313–318.

The above findings about the *social* variables in individual learners' lives tell us more about their language learning than the instruments designed to investigate motivation, and there are similarities between these findings and those of Norton (2000), so it is a good idea to turn to Reading 1 now. Although the methodology was different, the research described in this reading also found that those learners who manage to gain access to social networks in which English is spoken are likely to become more proficient in the language.

How do the learners described manage to achieve this access?

Language and culture are no longer scripts to be acquired, as much as they are conversations in which people can participate. The question of who is learning what and how much is essentially a question of what conversations they are part of, and this question is a subset of the more powerful question of what conversations are around to be had in a given culture. (McDermott, 1993, p. 295)

The notion of *best practices* has been a preoccupation in a variety of professional fields including education, management, business, health care, and social work. In the field of second language acquisition (SLA), interest in discovering and disseminating information about successful activities or practices has had a long history. Carroll (1967) urged investigation of the learning biographies of persons who had been successful in learning more than one language, and Stern (1975), Rubin (1975), and Cohen (1977) all speculated about distinctive learning strategies of good language learners. A particularly influential study on the characteristics and learning strategies of successful language learners, *The Good Language Learner* (*The GLL*; Naiman, Fröhlich, Stern, & Todesco, 1978), was undertaken in the mid-1970s. This study anticipated many of the issues and questions that preoccupied SLA researchers in the 1980s (see, e.g., Ellis, 1986; Johnson & Newport, 1989; Long, 1985; O'Malley & Chamot, 1990; Oxford, 1989). Indeed, these studies of good language learners provide a window on theories of SLA dominant at the time. This Forum piece, focusing as it does on our more recent research on good language learners, provides an opportunity to assess not only changing conceptions of good language learners but current trends in SLA theory.

We first examine Naiman *et al.*'s (1978) study as representative of several SLA studies of good language learning. We outline its theoretical foundations and methodological approaches. We then briefly examine more recent sociocultural and poststructural theory, developed mainly but not exclusively within the disciplinary boundaries of psychology, sociology, anthropology, and feminist theory, as relevant to the study of good language learning. We draw on our own more recent research on two good language learners – one adult (Eva) and one child (Julie) – and a comparison of the cases. By focussing on the situated experiences of these two learners, we seek new insights into the dialectic between the individual and the social; between the human agency of these learners and the social practices of their communities.

In seeking such insights, we are not suggesting that earlier researchers were not interested in social context. In much SLA research, as in the good language learner studies, researchers referred to *context*, or the environment of L2 learning, but as Davis (1995) points out was common in work from this perspective, context was seen as at most a modifier of the internal activity that occurred in individual language learners. The questions of interest were how good learners approached language learning tasks differently from poor learners and what characteristics of learners predisposed them to good or poor learning. Further, the work of such sociolinguistic researchers as Wolfson and Judd (1983), for example, was linguistically rather than anthropologically motivated. Hence their linguistic analysis of speech acts such as apologies and compliments, male/female language, and *foreigner talk*. We argue for approaches to good language learning that focus not only on learners' internal characteristics, learning strategies, or linguistic outputs but also on the reception of their actions in particular sociocultural communities.

SLA research and good language learning

The GLL (Naiman et al., 1978) appeared at a time when researchers such as Carroll (1967), Rubin (1975), Stern (1975), and Cohen (1977) were calling for research to test the hypothesis that successful learners were somehow different in constitution from poorer learners and that they engaged in particular facilitating activities while learning languages. Examining the experiences of adults and children defined as good language learners by themselves, by their teachers, or by performance on language proficiency measures, the intent of *The GLL* was to discover if successful learners had particular constellations of personality characteristics, cognitive styles, attitudes, motivations, or past learning experiences that were different from those of less successful learners. In addition to examining characteristics conceptualized as internal to the individual learner, the study's authors were interested in determining learner strategies, techniques, and activities that correlated with success in language learning.

The GLL had two parts. The first concerned adults who had learned a variety of languages, and the second concerned Canadian schoolchildren learning French as an L2. The adult subjects' descriptions of their learning activities and experiences were correlated with self-reports of their language learning success. The authors summarized the results of these correlations, noting that adult good language learners appeared to use five significant strategies: (a) taking an active approach to the task of language learning, (b) recognizing and exploiting the systematic nature of language, (c) using the language they were learning for communication and interaction, (d) managing their own affective difficulties with language learning, and (e) monitoring their language learning performance.

The child study component of *The GLL*, which correlated a large number of language proficiency measures with measures of personality, attitude, and cognitive style, confirmed the authors' hypothesis that certain aspects of learner characteristics were more significantly correlated with language learning success than others were. However, the authors also found that the "majority of the cognitive style and personality tests administered did not yield any systematic relationships to the criterion measures [results on the proficiency tests]". Rather than questioning the hypothesis that specific personality and cognitive traits were correlated with achievement, the researchers speculated about the possibility of low construct validity in the tests they used; they concluded that better measures for personality factors needed to be found or constructed. However, the authors found that their study confirmed findings of previous studies that "attitude and motivation were in many instances the best overall predictors of success in second language learning".

Many subsequent SLA studies of adults and children (Bailey, 1983; Bialystok, 1990; Chamot & O'Malley, 1994; Dulay, Burt, & Krashen, 1982; Ellis, 1989; Gardner, Day, & MacIntyre, 1992; Huang & Hatch, 1978; Saville-Troike, 1988; Strong, 1983; Wong Fillmore, 1979) were conducted on the basis of assumptions that learners had particular cognitive traits, affective orientations, motivations, past experiences, and other individual characteristics, and that they used particular individual learning strategies, all of which affected their L2 learning. In an early SLA study, for example, Wong Fillmore (1979) suggested the following in the case of a successful child L2 learner: "The secret of Nora's spectacular success as a language learner can be found in the special combination of interests, inclinations, skills, temperament, needs and motivations that comprised her personality".

In sum, as Larsen-Freeman observed in a survey of SLA research in 1991, SLA researchers until then had been preoccupied with discovering the cognitive processes of language acquisition and the effects of learners' characteristics on these processes. L2 learning, from this perspective, was the process by which individual learners (with certain characteristics) internalized language forms in interaction with available L2 input. SLA research was concerned with discovering how these individual learners managed their interactions with L2 input and organized their L2 output. In this way, as Naiman et al. (1978) suggested, language learning was described as mental processes such as "perceiving, analyzing, classifying, relating, storing, retrieving, and constructing a language output". The situated experience of learners was not a focus of such research. To investigate such experience, we draw on more recent theory and research.

. . .

Identifying two "good" language learners

We now examine aspects of studies we independently conducted with cohorts of language learners in the 1990s (Norton, 2000; Norton Peirce, 1995; Toohey, 1996, 1998, 2000). Norton's work was with adults; Toohey's with children. Both studies were qualitative and used a variety of data-gathering techniques: journals and interviews (in the adult study) and participant observation, interviews, and videotaping (in the child study). Both involved data gathering in multiple sites over significant periods of time – 1 year in the adult study and 3 years in the child study. Both employed critical research methods in interpreting their data. In both cases, we were less interested in the internal characteristics of the learners than in the characteristics of their social interactions as well as the practices in the communities in which they were learning English.

In the adult study (Norton, 2000), conducted with five immigrant women in Canada, one language learner, Eva, a young Polish woman, could be considered more successful than the others. During the course of the study, the five learners were assessed by means of a cloze passage, dictation, dialogue, crossword, short essay, and oral interview. Although each of the learners had arrived in Canada with little experience speaking English, Eva's performance on these measures was outstanding relative to that of the other learners. In terms of her knowledge of particular language forms, she was unequivocally a good language learner. What is perplexing, however, is that all five learners could be considered good language learners in terms of the strategies identified in *The GLL*. Each of them took an active approach to the task of language learning; they all recognized and exploited the systematicity of language; they used their language for communication and inter-action; they managed their affective difficulties with language learning; and they all monitored their language learning performance. How was it, then, that Eva had proved particularly effective as a language learner? She lived in a neighborhood in which little English was spoken, and her partner, Janus, was Polish. One clue to the answer to this question, we believe, lies in the extent to which Eva was able to negotiate entry into the anglophone social networks in her workplace, Munchies, despite initial difficulties.

The second learner to be considered is Julie, who was at the time reported here the 5-year-old child of Polish-speaking immigrant parents. Julie had not attended an English preschool program, but she and her younger sister had attended a Polish-medium Sunday school since they were quite young. Julie (as well as five other children of minority language backgrounds) was observed in a public school over the course of 3 years from the beginning of kindergarten to the end of Grade 2, for a study aimed at discovering how these children came to be participants in school activities (Toohey, 2000). Julie was initially identified as an ESL learner on the basis of an interview with her kindergarten teacher before school entrance, and she subsequently attended a supplementary afternoon ESL kindergarten with ESL children from other classes. By the end of kindergarten, her teacher assessed her as being enough like (in the teacher's words) a "normal" (i.e., English-speaking) child linguistically and academically that she would have a good year in Grade 1; the teacher also predicted that Julie would not require any special assistance with ESL. In view of her mother's opinion that Julie started school speaking Polish appro-priately for her age but that she knew only "a few words [of English] . . . not much," her progress seemed extraordinary. No formal English proficiency tests were administered to the children by the school or as part of the study described here, but Julie's teacher's assessment of her as academically and linguistically able, and the evidence that she participated in a wide variety of classroom interactions, are the basis for the selection of her experience as a relevant case of good language learning. Psychologically derived models might hypothesize that Julie had particular cognitive traits, motivations, and strategies that led to her success in language learning. Like Eva's, however, Julie's success evidently was at least partially determined by the structure and characteristics of the practices in her classroom and the social relationships permitted and negotiated therein.

Practices and agency in diverse settings

With reference to the good language learners in our respective studies, we draw on social, anthropological, and critical theory to approach two central questions: (a) How did the practices in the environments of these good language learners constrain or facilitate their access to English, and (b) how did these good language learners gain access to the social networks of their communities? We see these questions as a dialectic between the constraints and possibilities offered by the learners' environments and their agency as learners.

Community practices

With respect to the first question, we need to examine how language, work, and schooling practices were structured. Munchies, a fast-food restaurant, was a workplace that had differentiated practices for workers, and lengthy conversations between coworkers or between workers and customers were unusual (except at the tea-time breaks, when coworkers would chat with one another). Workers needed to satisfy customers' requests as expeditiously and efficiently as possible, and even servers, who were encouraged to communicate politely, engaged in only brief exchanges. Some tasks, like cleaning the floors or emptying garbage, were solitary and required little or no language. The desirability of jobs in the restaurant (not only for an English language learner like Eva) was in direct relationship to the level of interaction they necessitated, and those people who performed solitary jobs were considered less desirable than other workers. Cleaning the floors, unfortunately, was seen as a suitable job for an immigrant, a newcomer, and an English language learner. Eva's positioning in these tasks blocked her access to conversations with her coworkers and limited her opportunities to engage in community practices like talking while working. Eva did have access to tea-time conversations, but they were not very lengthy, and they required expertise at linguistic practices that Eva, as a relatively inexperienced speaker of English, did not have. If Eva's English proficiency had been tested at this point, when her workplace community had blocked her access to practice with more experienced participants, she might not have appeared a good language learner.

However, the workplace community of practice overlapped with another community of practice, the social contacts in which workers participated outside work. It was company policy at Munchies that the management would help sponsor a monthly outing for employees. At these times Eva was taken outside the workplace, where she had been positioned as a "stupid" person, only worthy of the "worst kind of job," as she put it, to a context in which her youth and charm were valued symbolic resources. On these occasions Eva's partner would help provide transportation for her fellow employees. Outside the institutional constraints of the workplace, where the nature of the work undertaken by Munchies employees structured to a large extent the social relations of power in the workplace, a different set of relationships began to develop. Eva's identity in the eyes of her coworkers became more complex, and their relationship to her began to change. As Eva explained,

> For example yesterday when we went out, the manager she said to me – because I am just one year younger than she – "You look really different when you are not at work." Because when I am at the work I – when I do the hard job – I don't know, I'm different than like here.

Her subsequent reassignment to other jobs in the restaurant allowed her to speak, and to speak from a more desirable position. In this case, therefore, whereas some workplace practices constrained her access to and participation in speaking English, others permitted her access; in time, space was made for her to participate more actively in the social and verbal activities of her community.

Practices in workplaces, linguistic and otherwise, are different from practices in schools, where talk is often seen to be integral to the job of classroom learning. Julie's kindergarten teacher encouraged the children to talk, share ideas, listen to stories, and give opinions, and play was an explicit component of the curriculum. At Circle Time, the teacher asked children to participate in choral activities to whatever extent they wished, and their participation there was heavily scaffolded by their teacher and the other children. Solo contributions at Circle Time were also scaffolded by their teacher. In play, children were together, and they might or might not speak to one another while manipulating classroom material resources. Few activities in the kindergarten were solitary, and language did not seem to be the most important mediator of social activity. This is not to say that all children had easy access to peers, play, and play resources; at times some children were forcefully excluded from these, and exclusion was as clearly much a classroom practice as scaffolded inclusion was. However, Julie was rarely excluded by other children, and she had allies, both child and adult, who protected her right to participate. The practices of Julie's kindergarten classroom aided her in participating more and more actively in the social and verbal activities of the community.

The contrasting practices of Eva's and Julie's communities explain, in part, why Eva's route to participation seemed more fraught with difficulty than Julie's. Although both Eva and Julie were accountable to more experienced members of their institutional hierarchies, in the form of the manager and the teacher, respectively, Eva's relationship to her manager was very different from Julie's relationship to her teacher. Eva's boss did not consider the development of Eva's communication skills as an institutional responsibility. Although the boss may have sought to make better use of Eva's improving communication skills, the responsibility was on Eva to demonstrate that she was sufficientiy competent to undertake linguistically challenging tasks. In Julie's case, in contrast, the teacher saw it as her responsibility to help Julie and the other English learners improve their English skills; she provided much scaffolding in the learning process and gave these children many opportunities to talk. Further, although Eva's boss was centrally concerned with Eva's productivity as a worker, the teacher had multidimensional expectations of Julie as a student. She was interested not only in learning outcomes but in Julie's behaviour in class and her relationship with peers. Whereas Eva struggled to be given more desirable jobs in the restaurant, jobs that required the newly acquired skill of using English, in which she was heard to be deficient, Julie's participation in English language activities was encouraged and scaffolded.

Human agency

Our second question concerns how these language learners – ultimately good learners – exercised human agency to gain access to the social networks of their communities. Both learners were exposed to English in an institutional context in which English was the major means of communication. Eva was the only Polish speaker in her workplace, and Julie's kindergarten classroom, though enrolling children of diverse language backgrounds, included only two other speakers of Polish, both boys, with whom Julie seldom interacted. For Eva and Julie, access to peers was important not only for language learning but for social affiliation. What is remarkable in both cases is that even though attempts were made to subordinate or isolate the learners, both made effective use of a variety of resources to gain access to their peer networks. Two such resources can be described as intellectual and social, respectively.

With regard to intellectual resources, Eva, for example, drew on her knowledge of Italian as well as her knowledge of other countries to contribute to conversations with her peers. One of her coworkers who had an Italian husband was very happy to learn some basic Italian from Eva, and other coworkers were impressed by her knowledge of European countries – which are considered desirable travel desti-nations in Canada. In a very different context, Julie also sometimes tried to teach Polish to peers, and the data illustrate how she used her access to proprietary information (secrets) to resist subordination and to position herself as a desirable playmate with access to valued information. Julie also knew, in effect, school secrets: Her participation in Polish Sunday school for several years had made her familiar with classroom routines, materials, and expected demeanor. In both Eva's and Julie's cases, the reception for their intellectual offerings was positive. Although both exerted agency in making these offerings, the others in their social context determined the worth of their contributions. Again, an interaction between the agency of the learners and the social frameworks in which they exercised that agency is evident.

With regard to social resources, both Eva and Julie had community or extra-community allies to position themselves more favorably within their peer networks. On management outings, Eva's partner not only provided rides for her coworkers but helped position Eva as someone in a desirable relationship. Julie developed both adult and child allies at school, most noteworthy of which was her cousin Agatha, an experienced speaker of English and Polish. Such relationships served to place Eva and Julie in more powerful positions with respect to their peers, enhancing their opportunities to participate in the conversations around them. Had Eva's boyfriend or Julie's allies not been seen as desirable, Eva and Julie might not have been able to negotiate more desirable places for themselves and more opportunities for verbal and social interaction.

Past approaches to explaining good language learners might assume that Eva and Julie had gradually developed appropriate strategies for interaction in their respective linguistic communities by, for example, monitoring their performance more diligently and exploiting the target language more systematically. Our research paints a far more complex picture, however. Rather than focussing on language structures per se, both learners sought to set up counterdiscourses in which their identities could be respected and their resources valued, thereby enhancing the possibilities for shared conversation. Eva, initially constructed as an ESL immigrant, sought to reposition herself as a multilingual resource with a desirable partner; Julie, initially constructed as an ESL learner, came to be seen as a nice little girl with allies. Their success in claiming more powerful identities seems important to their success as good language learners. This is not to say that proficiency in English was irrelevant in the process of accessing peer networks, particularly in Eva's case, but rather that struggles over identity were central.

Conclusion

In this commentary we have argued that the proficiencies of the good language learners in our studies were bound up not only in what they did individually but also in the possibilities their various communities offered them. Our research and recent theoretical discussions have convinced us that understanding good language learning requires attention to social practices in the contexts in which individuals learn L2s. As well, we have argued for the importance of examining the ways in which learners exercise their agency in forming and reforming their identities in those contexts. We see this dual focus as necessary to understand good language learning and as an important complement to earlier studies.

We conclude with a comment on the way conceptions of good language learners and SLA theory may evolve in the future. We believe it is significant that both Eva and Julie were able to access the social networks in their respective learning communities, albeit at different rates. We wonder what data we would have collected had Eva and Julie not been blonde and white-skinned, slim, able-bodied, well dressed, and attractive to Western eyes. In this regard, although Eva's coworkers were ultimately happy to work with her, they remained reluctant to work with other immigrants. And in the classroom, a South Asian girl was not as successful as Julie in resisting subordination. We hope that future research may lend important insight to issues of race, the body, and (good) language learning.

Norton and Toohey argue that their 'good language learners', Eva and Julie, are different from other learners in these studies because of the opportunities they had to enter into relationships with target language speakers. They were also different because they both had resources that enabled them to move from initially being perceived as powerless and undesirable in the eyes of these peers. In Norton's study of five adult learners, all had the psychological attributes described by Naiman *et al.* (see Norton (2000) for more details) but only Eva possessed the social access and cultural goods that would help her to become a member of the target community.

The role of the emotions

Another dimension of learning is the relationship between learning activity and our emotions, which are often labelled in SLA studies as the affective factor. Although emotions are ever-present in language-learning situations, they are not often the focus of research. For example, in the study by Khanna *et al.* (1998) in the previous section, feelings about the self and others are shown to be significant, but they are not investigated. In studies that do focus on the emotional dimensions of language learning, diary studies are the most common method of research. Kathleen Bailey, for instance, carried out a study of the relationship between anxiety and competitiveness in diaries kept by learners of foreign languages (see Allwright and Bailey, 1991, ch. 10).

Another study involving the use of diaries, by Rod Ellis, gives us some insight into the range of emotions experienced by language learners. In this study he focuses on metaphors used by both researchers and learners to describe the learning process, and points out the huge difference in the types of metaphors used (Ellis, 2001). In SLA studies metaphors for learning frequently construct the learning process as a mechanical one (input, output, uptake). If we go back to Breen's discussion of research in Reading 2, Chapter 1, he pins his argument on the significance of such metaphors in research into language learning, arguing that they are part of the way we construct our perceptions of processes that are not visible.

As part of his research Ellis analysed the journals of six adult learners on an intensive German as a foreign language course in London. The journals were kept for the first seven months of this beginner course. All six learners used metaphors that constructed language learning as a set of problems to solve, thus referring to the cognitive challenges they were facing. Five of them also represented their learning as suffering, recording experiences of anxiety, pain and hardship. These five also wrote of language learning as a journey, a path to be travelled at varying speeds. These were the main shared metaphors but there were individual variations in the ways the learners described their experiences and feelings. The study did not attempt to relate these descriptions to measurements of the progress in learning of the informants, but it serves to remind us of the personal pains and stress that are absent from constructions of learning as mechanical.

There do not yet appear to be any published studies of learning diaries kept by ESOL learners. However, Norton's study of five immigrant women discussed in Reading 1, and those described in the following chapters, give some indications of the complex range of emotions and feelings about the self that all such learners must experience as they learn the dominant language and strive to become 'good language learners'. Understanding the language-learning process remains incomplete if the emotional dimension is not taken into account.

Learner beliefs

All adult learners arrive in the language classroom with beliefs and opinions about the nature of formal education, and most have had some experience of schooling that has helped form these beliefs. Some of these beliefs may not coincide with teaching practices in UK classrooms, and this potential mismatch between teacher and learner beliefs may be a barrier to individual progress in additional language learning.

Beliefs about language learning

Exploring learner beliefs about formal learning practices can lead to change, as the following piece of research shows. In the Adult Migrant English Program (AMEP) in Australia two researchers and three teachers worked together on a project to investigate the everyday reading practices of small groups of Arabic-speaking, Chinese-speaking and Spanish-speaking learners (Burns and de Silva Joyce, 2000). The first aim of this study was to develop descriptions of how the learners used reading in their first languages during their daily lives. The second aim was to find out learner perceptions of reading activities in the classroom. One of the findings was that all the learners believed reading aloud was an important activity and would help them develop pronunciation and intonation, although it was not part of classroom practice. Interestingly, the practice of reading aloud was mentioned by many learners from different backgrounds. It seemed to be a widely shared belief, and raises the question (which we will return to below) about the cultural basis of many so-called individual attributes and learning approaches.

In a related project, three other teachers drew on the findings of the reading practice study to experiment with classroom reading activities. For example, they organized small reading groups in which graded readers were discussed and read aloud. The learners participating in these activities all responded positively and felt they had made progress in reading and pronunciation. Thus in this research teachers explored the beliefs and practices of learners and adapted some of their classroom practices. Accordingly, the project is an example which supports the argument that Breen goes on to make in his discussion of the classroom as culture, that 'teaching language and investigating language learning may be seen to be synonymous' (Breen, 2001, p. 137).

Differences in ways of knowing

An American study of learner beliefs by developmental psychologists has taken a different path from the Australian research. This study set out to trace how learners' perceptions of their learning and meaning-making changed as they progressed through a language programme (Kegan *et al.*, 2001). It was based on a body of knowledge about the psychological development of adults' *ways of knowing* through which, it is argued, an individual makes sense of her experiences. These ways of knowing are categorized as Instrumental, Socializing and Self-authoring. Briefly, a person who makes meaning through an Instrumental way of knowing tends to be guided by rules and observable actions and behaviours. Those with a Socializing way of knowing understand their own identity through their relationships with other people and ideas. Those with a Self-authoring way of knowing take responsibility for their own systems of belief and feelings of self. They are seen as developmental stages through which adults develop very gradually, with Self-authoring being the most complex and desirable set of perceptions and beliefs.

The learners involved in this research comprised forty-one ABE/ESOL students on three different adult programmes: a family literacy course, a high school diploma course run on a workplace site and a pre-enrolment ESOL course for higher education. The programmes were chosen because they were considered by the researchers to be sites of best practice, and also because each included not only language learning (or general education on the workplace site) but also aimed to enhance 'adults' specific role competency in one of three social roles: student, parent or worker'. Their informants came from many countries, and ranged from newly arrived learners in the preparation for the higher education course to those learners who had been in the USA for up to twenty years in the workplace course.

The researchers visited each site three times over nine months plus an additional visit to the workplace site where the course lasted fourteen months. On each visit they conducted open-ended interviews with each informant. Questions included 'What are your purposes in pursuing this learning?' and 'What, in your view, makes a person a good teacher?' These interviews were conducted in English due to budget limitations. Structured exercises and surveys were also administered, and classroom observations and focus groups were conducted.

The research found a diversity in the ways of knowing on each of the programmes which was virtually identical with comparable samples of American English-speaking adults, and they also found that differences in ways of knowing did not have any significant relationships with levels of experience with formal education. Thus some learners with little previous formal education demonstrated developmentally complex meaning systems. Over the research period it was found that all the informants gained new knowledge and self-confidence, and some developed more complex ways of knowing. Those who made progress in transforming their ways of knowing also changed their conceptions of what it meant to be a good student or a good parent, or what a good teacher was.

One finding that the researchers had not expected from this research was the importance of the learner peer group across all three sites. All informants reported that their academic learning was enhanced through participating in collaborative learning activities, and that being part of a learner group helped them to broaden their perspectives. Their peers were also reported to provide emotional and psychological support. The groups were likened to a 'family' or a 'band of warriors' or 'fellow strugglers'. Although this research was designed to focus on individual progress and learning processes, the learners themselves brought into the discussion the social nature of their learning.

This study gives us some valuable insights into the learning processes of individuals in classrooms, and provides one way of understanding the relationships between belief and language learning. However, there are some problems with its methodology and underlying assumptions that we can learn from. First, the informants in this study were required to talk about their beliefs about language learning in the language they were in the process of learning. We cannot know what meanings were lost to this study because the learners could not express them in English.

Second, there is no discussion of 'observer effect'. The informants were interviewed in the dominant language by outside experts whose social status may well have seemed higher than the status of the students. It is possible that some informants could have been attempting to supply what they perceived the researchers wanted to hear, or they could have suppressed some responses as appearing impolite. There is no discussion of such potential problems, or any indication that these problems were taken into account in the analysis of the findings.

The researchers also seemed to wholeheartedly embrace the objectives of each of the programmes visited that were about social rather than language learning goals: 'each [programme] oriented to enhancing greater English language fluency, increasing content knowledge and improving effectiveness as workers, parents, or students' (Keegan *et al.*, 2001: 2). There is no exploration of the deficit view of the social roles of additional language learners that is implicit in this description, or awareness that some adult learners may resist being positioned in this way. For example, when discussing learners on the family literacy programme categorized as Instrumental knowers (the first developmental stage), one example they gave as illustrating this way of knowing was that such learners 'often found it difficult to put themselves in the shoes of their children and understood proper discipline as ensuring their children did what they were told, followed the rules, and met parental needs' (Keegan *et al.*, 2001: 9). Such a response to questions about effective parenting could be part of an adult's resistance to the ideology of parenting that dominated the programme, rather than stemming from a particular way of knowing. It could also reflect difference in cultural attitudes, as I discuss below.

📖 *Activity: Guided Reading*

Reading 2:

Chamot, A. (2001) 'The role of learning strategies in second language acquisition' in Breen, M. (ed.) *Learner Contributions to Language Learning: New Directions in Research*, Harlow: Longman, pp. 25–35, 40–41.

There is no examination of cultural differences in the study above, despite the fact that the informants are said to have come from 'every part of the world'. The three ways of knowing are presented as universal to all adults, yet it could be argued that they reflect particular Western beliefs about learning. For example, the most desirable way of knowing is presented as the Self-authoring way. An essential characteristic of this category is autonomy: 'Self-Authoring knowers took greater responsibility for their learning both inside and outside of the classroom'.

Such active learning is certainly part of the definition of a 'good language learner' in studies referred to by Chamot in Reading 2 of this chapter. Yet Chamot ends her review of the teaching and learning of learning strategies with questions as yet unanswered. Among these is one about the cultural nature of definitions of good learning practices. She asks, 'Are learning strategies that seek to develop learner autonomy perceived as valuable universally or only in some cultures?' (Chamot, 2001: 42). This is not a question asked by the researchers of this American study. I suggest you read the extract of Chamot's discussion of research into learning strategies now.

As you read, keep in mind Chamot's question above: Are learning strategies universal or part of particular cultures?

Introduction

An important contribution that learners make to acquiring a second language is their use of learning strategies – the techniques or procedures that facilitate a learning task. Learning strategies are directed towards a goal and, as mental procedures, are not directly observable, though some learning strategies may result in specific behaviours. For example, an individual might decide to attend to certain aspects of incoming information, such as listening for a specific event or time, or scanning a text to find a particular piece of information. This selective attention is a learning strategy that has the goal of understanding, storing or retrieving information. During the process of selective attention, the individual may also decide to write down important information for future reference or as a memory aid. Thus, note-taking is an observable learning strategy paired with the unobservable strategy of selective attention. Students who try to take notes without deciding to attend selectively to specific aspects of input quickly fall behind as they try to write down everything they are listening to or copy everything they are reading.

Learning strategies are important in second language acquisition for two major reasons. First, in investigating the strategies used by second language learners during the language learning process, we gain insights into the cognitive, social and affective processes involved in language learning. These insights can help us understand these mental processes as they relate to second language acquisition, and can also clarify similarities and differences between language learning and general learning processes. The second reason supporting research into language learning strategies is that it may be possible to teach less successful language learners to use the strategies that characterize their more successful peers, thus helping students who are experiencing difficulty in learning a second language become better language learners. Therefore, two major goals in language learning strategy research are to (1) identify and compare the learning strategies used by more and less successful language learners, and (2) provide instruction to less successful language learners that helps them become more successful in their language study.

In order to achieve these goals, the first step is to gain a clear understanding of the learning strategies used by language learners and differences between learning strategies of more and less effective learners. The second step is to find the most effective approach to teaching language learning strategies. Finally, we need to discover whether instruction in language learning strategies actually has an impact on proficiency and achievement in the second language.

This chapter first provides a brief overview of methods used by various researchers to identify language learning strategies and discuss the strengths and weaknesses of each. The second section presents representative learning strategies studies in first language contexts, and discusses aspects of this body of research that have applications to second language learning. This is followed by an overview of major studies of learning strategies in second language acquisition research. . . . The final section is a summary of what we have learned about language learning strategies, and suggestions for moving forward in this area of research.

How are learning strategies investigated?

In the more than twenty years of investigation of language learning strategies, researchers have used a variety of approaches for identifying the mental processes used by learners as they seek to understand, remember and use a new language. Observation of students in language classrooms has proved singularly fruitless as a method of identifying learning strategies (Cohen, 1998; Naiman et al., 1978, 1996; O'Malley and Chamot, 1990; Rubin, 1975; Wenden, 1991a). The reason why classroom observation yields little information about students' use of learning strategies is that most learning strategies are mental processes and as such are not directly observable in terms of outward behaviour. Therefore, research in this area has relied for the most part on learners' self-reports. These self-reports have been made through retrospective interviews, stimulated recall interviews, questionnaires, written diaries and journals, and think-aloud protocols concurrent with a learning task. Each of these methods has limitations, but at the present time the only way to gain any insight at all into the unobservable mental learning strategies of learners is by asking them to reveal their thinking processes.

In retrospective interviews, learners are asked to reflect on a learning task and recall what strategies or 'special tricks' they used to carry out the task (see O'Malley et al., 1985a). The task may be a recently completed one or a typical task with which the learner is familiar, such as learning and remembering new vocabulary words or reading a story in the target language. The questions asked may be open-ended ('What do you do when you are reading and you see an unfamiliar word?') or specific ('When you are reading and see an unfamiliar word, do you make inferences about the meaning or just read on?'). The advantages of retrospective interviews are that they provide a great deal of flexibility, as the interviewer can clarify the questions if necessary, ask follow-up questions and comment on the student's responses. In addition, if the retrospective interview is conducted with a small group of three or four students, one student's comments can spur the memories of other students about their uses of learning strategies. The disadvantages of retrospective interviews are that students may not report their strategy use accurately, that they may report what they perceive as the interviewer's preferred answers, or that they may claim to use strategies that have been encouraged by teachers rather than actually used by students.

A stimulated recall interview is more likely to accurately reveal students' learning strategies because it is conducted immediately after the student has engaged in a learning task. The actual task is videotaped, the interviewer then plays back the videotape, pausing as necessary, and asks the student to describe his or her thoughts at that specific moment during the learning task (Robbins, 1996). Studying learning strategies through stimulated recall interviews can produce task-specific strategy descriptions with corroborating evidence of their use. However, this method is time-consuming and only yields the strategies used on one occasion for a specific task. It does not reveal the range of students' strategies or their frequency across tasks.

Questionnaires are the easiest way to collect data about students' reported use of learning strategies and questionnaires such as Oxford's Strategy Inventory for Language Learning (SILL) have been used extensively to collect data on large numbers of language learners (Oxford, 1996c). The SILL is a standardized measure with versions for ESL students and students of a variety of foreign languages and, as such, is extremely useful for collecting and analysing information about large numbers of students. Other studies have developed questionnaires focused on particular learning activities in which their subjects were engaged (Chamot and Küpper, 1989; O'Malley et al., 1985a). One of the advantages of questionnaires aside from their ease of administration, is that students are asked to rate the frequency with which they use a particular strategy, rather than only indicating whether they use it at all. The drawbacks of questionnaires are that students may not understand the intent of a question that they may answer according to their perception of the 'right answer', and that the questionnaire may not fully elicit all of a student's strategies.

A think-aloud protocol involves a one-on-one interview in which the language learner is given a target language task and asked to describe his or her thoughts while working on it. The interviewer may prompt with open-ended questions such as, 'What are you thinking right now? Why did you stop and start over?' Think-aloud interviews are recorded and transcribed verbatim, then analysed for evidence of learning strategies. While think-aloud procedures often provide a very clear picture of a learner's on-line processing strategies, they also have shortcomings. These include the presence of the interviewer and the somewhat artificial situation, which may affect the learner's responses. For example, the learner may not engage in his or her usual amount of planning before engaging in the task because of a perception that the interviewer wants the task to be completed quickly. Similarly, once the task is completed, the learner may not (without a direct prompt) take the time to look back on the task and evaluate his or her performance. An additional drawback of think-aloud procedures is that individual interviews, transcription, and analysis are extraordinarily labour-intensive. In spite of these difficulties, however, data collected through think-aloud protocols provide rich insights into language-learning strategies.

Research on self-reports of the use of learning strategies has provided important information about learners' understanding of their own learning processes. However, a weakness in learning strategy research is that all data collection methods are subjective in nature, depending as they do on self-report from the learner. A second area of research on learning strategies has examined approaches to teaching students effective strategies for a variety of learning tasks. This second area has been most thoroughly investigated in first-language contexts.

. . .

What do descriptive studies of language learning strategies reveal?

Research on language learning strategies has focused mainly on descriptive studies that have identified characteristics of 'the good language learner' and compared the strategies of more effective and less effective language learners. These studies have been important in understanding how language learners use strategies, and they have provided important information to guide experimental studies to identify the effects of learning strategies instruction on students.

Descriptive studies of language learning strategies have taken several forms. This line of research began with studies of the characteristics of effective language learners. As the role of strategies became clear, researchers began developing instruments for measuring students' strategies use. Other studies have used individual, group, or think-aloud interviews to characterize how students apply strategies while working on language learning tasks. These descriptive studies include comparisons of learning strategies used by more and less effective language learners and, more recently, studies of how learning strategies develop over time.

Who is the 'good language learner'?

In 1975, Rubin suggested that a model of 'the good language learner' could be identified by looking at special strategies used by students who were successful in their second language learning. Stern (1975) also identified a number of learner characteristics and strategic techniques associated with good language learners. Hosenfeld (1976) further elaborated these characteristics, using think-aloud protocols, to investigate students' mental processes while they worked on language tasks. These studies were followed by the work of Naiman, Fröhlich, Stern and Todesco (1978, 1996), which further pursued the notion that second language learning ability resided at least in part in the strategies one uses for learning. Taken together, these studies identified the good language learner as one who is an active learner, monitors language production, practises communicating in the language, makes use of prior linguistic knowledge, uses various memorization techniques, and asks questions for clarification.

. . .

What strategies do learners use during language tasks?

While questionnaires such as the SILL are useful for gathering information from large numbers of subjects for quantitative comparisons, in-depth interview studies have elicited rich descriptions of students' use of learning strategies. For example, in a longitudinal EFL study, Robbins (1996) investigated the learning strategies of Japanese college students as they developed their ability to carry on conversations in English. Paired with a native speaker of English, the Japanese students were videotaped before and after an eight-month period of language exchange. The students watched videotapes of their conversations and provided a verbal report on their thoughts during them. Despite their reputation for reticence, the students reported their thought processes, and therefore their learning strategies, in great detail. It was found that fewer learning strategies were reported as the students progressed towards being more at ease with conversation in English; probably because of fewer challenges and pauses to recall the problem when reviewing the conversation. Some students mentioned that the experience of watching themselves converse on video made them more aware of what aspects of their speaking ability they needed to improve.

An early study of seventy high school ESL students identified the range and variety of learning strategies used for different tasks by successful students. The study revealed that these good language learners were active and strategic, and could focus on the requirements of a task, reflect on their own learning processes, and transfer previously learned concepts and learning strategies to the demands of the English as a second language (ESL) or general education content classroom (Chamot, 1987; O'Malley et al., 1985a).

Do more and less language effective learners use strategies differently?

A follow-up investigation to O'Malley, Chamot, Stewner-Manzanares, Küpper and Russo (1985a) compared the learning strategy profiles of more and less successful students in ESL classrooms and discovered significant differences in the listening approaches of the two groups (O'Malley et al., 1989). The more effective students *monitored* their comprehension by asking themselves if what they were hearing made sense, they related new information to their own *prior knowledge*, and they made *inferences* about possible meanings when encountering unfamiliar words. In addition, the more successful students were able to transfer their prior academic knowledge in Spanish to the requirements of the English-language classroom. Thus, these more effective ESL listeners were displaying a number of learning strategies that are typical of good readers in native English-speaking contexts (e.g., Pressley et al., 1995).

The body of research on second language reading and writing processes also includes descriptions and comparisons of strategy use by more and less effective readers and writers (see, for example, Barnett, 1988: Cohen and Cavalcanti, 1990; Devine, 1993; Krapels, 1990). This research indicates that good second language readers are able to monitor their comprehension and take action when comprehension falters, and that composing strategies are more important than language proficiency in good second language writing.

A study of high school foreign language students used individual, group, and think-aloud interviews in which students identified the learning strategies they used for a variety of language tasks, including listening, reading, grammar cloze, role-playing and writing (Chamot et al., 1988a; Chamot, Dale et al., 1993). Differences between more and less effective learners were found in the number and range of strategies used, in how the strategies were applied to the task, and in whether they were appropriate for the task. In these studies, students' understanding of the task's requirements and whether they could match a strategy to meet those requirements seemed to be a major determinant of effective use of learning strategies.

Other studies comparing more and less effective language students have revealed a recurring finding that less successful learners do use learning strategies, sometimes even as frequently as their more successful peers, but that the strategies are used differently (Abraham and Vann, 1987; Chamot and El-Dinary, 1999; Chamot et al., 1988b; Keatley et al., 1999; Padron and Waxman, 1988; Vandergrift, 1997a, 1997b; Vann and Abraham, 1990). These studies confirmed that good language learners demonstrated adeptness at matching strategies to the task they were working on, while the less successful language learners seemed to lack the metacognitive knowledge about task requirements needed to select appropriate strategies. This trend was apparent with children in foreign language immersion classrooms, high school ESL and foreign language students, and adult language learners.

. . .

What are the next steps for language learning strategies research?

The study of language learning strategies will continue to develop as second language acquisition researchers seek to understand different learner characteristics and the complex cognitive, social and affective factors involved in processing language input and using the language for a variety of purposes. Likewise, language educators and methodologists will continue their quest for more effective instructional approaches and, with the increasing emphasis on learner-centred instruction and learner empowerment in all areas of education, instruction in learning strategies will assume a greater role in teacher preparation and curriculum design. How successful future research in language learning strategies will be depends in large part on the development and adaptation of instruments that are reliable and valid in identifying the strategies (whether acquired independently or through instruction) that learners use, and on the design of research studies that address questions that as yet have not been answered. Weaknesses in current research on language learning strategies include those related to research methodology and to unanswered questions about developmental stages and individual and cultural variations in the acquisition and use of strategies.

How should research methodology be improved?

As described earlier in this chapter, the instruments used to collect data on language learning strategies are all based on learners' self-reports. At present there does not seem to be any other possible approach, since behavioural observation is not an effective way to identify internal mental processes. However, the instruments used to collect verbal reports can certainly be strengthened. Questionnaires, for example, can be made more context-specific to include questions about language learning tasks that students are actually engaged in. Questionnaires that include a large number of items referring to unfamiliar learning experiences are difficult for respondents to understand and answer accurately. In a communicative language classroom, students would provide more accurate information on a questionnaire that asks questions about learning strategies framed within descriptions of typical communicative activities. Similarly, students from different language and cultural backgrounds would probably respond with greater understanding to questions that reflect their own learning experiences and educational or cultural values. In addition, learning strategy questionnaires need to be developed for different developmental stages and ages of students, including adaptations for students with low levels of literacy in both the L1 and the L2. Once such learner and context-specific learning strategy questionnaires are developed, they need to be standardized on a large group of the types of student for whom they are intended. Similar types of standardization procedure need to be developed for interview protocols that reflect factors such as age, L1 and type of language program.

Another methodological challenge in much of the research is the establishment of a correlation between the use of learning strategies and increased proficiency and achievement in the target language. Many researchers have had to rely on teacher or researcher-constructed tests of language proficiency to show that students who use learning strategies learn more effectively than students who do not use strategies. Often the reason is that the research is conducted on beginning-level students, and standardized tests do not distinguish small differences in proficiency in beginning-level students. Another difficulty with language tests is that the test-taking or language proficiency interview situations may actually discourage the use of learning strategies, as these typically call for responses that have been learned to the point of automaticity and there is little time available to applying learning strategies (rapid recall strategies might be the exception). A better language test might be one in which the learner is given time to solve a language learning problem rather than having to perform quickly and correctly on a language task.

In addition to refining the instruments used in learning strategy research, research designs need to include multiple sources of data, both quantitative and qualitative, as the convergence of evidence strengthens claims to causal effects. Since language learning is a slow process, studies of the effects of learning strategies need to be conducted over a long enough period of time for language gains to be demonstrated unequivocally. Finally, intervention studies need to include frequent observations of both the experimental and control classrooms to make certain that the teachers are indeed teaching the strategies, and that the control teachers are not in fact also teaching strategies! This type of sustained research effort brings with it a host of difficulties, but the results are more credible than very short studies and studies in which no control is exercised over instructional implementation.

Additional barriers to success in language learning

Trauma

One barrier to becoming a 'good language learner' is the trauma sadly experienced by some of the refugees and asylum seekers who arrive in the ESOL classroom. This trauma may be the result of torture, imprisonment, war experiences, long periods of time with very little food or perilous and arduous journeys (see Langer, 2002). Such experiences can have a negative effect on the person's language learning. The Canadian Centre for Victims of Torture (CCVT) has worked to provide details of such difficulties for those who have suffered torture (www.icomm. ca/ccvt). For example, survivors of torture are unable to concentrate for long periods of time, so CCVT recommends that class times are limited to no more than three hours per day with one or two breaks. (See also www.swsahs.nsw.gov.au/ areaser/Startts/links/imdex.asp for Australian advice on those who are suffering from trauma or who have undergone torture.)

In Sweden in 1991 a special course in Swedish as a second language was set up for refugees suffering from post-traumatic stress syndrome, after it was discovered that many of those learners dropping out of regular classes, or not making any progress in learning Swedish, were suffering from this condition. Language tuition on this course is combined with welfare support, counselling and, at a later stage, work experience. A description of this course is given by Jenny Roden in *Language Issues* (Roden, 1999), and the course has been evaluated through interviews with fifteen former participants (Carlson *et al.*, 2001). The report of this evaluation is not available in English at the time of writing. For a wider discussion on the effects of violence on learning, see Jenny Horsman (2001).

Dyslexia

Dyslexia is a learning disorder that has only recently received systematic attention, and this attention has been largely directed at those learning and using their first written language. So far, there is no body of research into how the disorder impedes the progress of the learner of an additional language. However, an ESOL and Dyslexia Working Party met for three years in England and produced a guide for ESOL teachers based on the experience of tutors practised in assessing and teaching bilingual and first language dyslexic learners (Sunderland *et al.*, 1997).

It is argued in this guide that dyslexia in a first language can have a considerable negative effect on additional language learning, because it is a condition which affects a person's language-processing abilities in three possible areas: auditory, visual or motor. Auditory difficulties will impede additional language learning because of problems in discriminating sounds, relating sounds to symbols and retrieving vocabulary. Visual processing difficulties can lead to reading problems and difficulties in ordering and sequencing. Motor-processing difficulties result in handwriting and spelling problems. Diagnosing and supporting ESOL dyslexic language learners is not an easy task, since tutors and learners need to ascertain which difficulties experienced by a learner are due to different cultural learning experiences, and which are specifically processing difficulties that the learner also experiences in her first language(s). For further reading see Peer and Reid (2000).

Difference: is it individual or social?

As you will see from the readings in this chapter, explorations of difference in the way learners approach the task of learning a language have traditionally focused on the individual, her attributes and strategies. These provide fruitful insights into the diverse ways language learning is undertaken. However, as this chapter shows, it is sometimes difficult or problematic to separate individual attributes, beliefs and strategies from the social and cultural environments where they are acquired or used. The two readings in this chapter give different pictures of language learners. Reading one explores strategies which adult learners may use or need outside of the classroom. Reading 2 takes account of the strategies which an ESOL learner may use, or be expected to use, in the UK classroom.

Activity: Discussion

Look back at the two readings
  What pictures do they paint of the learners they discuss? How are they different?

It could be argued (as does Breen) that we need to consider both individual and social factors of learning, and how they are intertwined in order to understand and support the language-learning journeys of ESOL learners.

Discussion

1. Chamot ends her review of research with some unanswered questions about learning strategies (not included in the extract in Reading 2). Among these, as I have already pointed out, she asks questions about the relationships between learning strategies and cultural beliefs and values. She says that more research is needed into the relationships between culture and language learning, and asks the following questions:

   'Are learning strategies that seek to develop learner autonomy perceived as valuable universally or only in some cultures?'

   'Are collaborative social strategies valued in competitive societies?' (see p. 55 of this book).

   - How do your teaching and/or personal language-learning experiences lead you to address these questions?
   - Should we teach learning strategies if they are a cultural rather than a universal phenomenon, or should we seek to build on the strategies familiar to our learners as in the Australian research discussed in this chapter?

2. In Reading 2, Chapter 1 (p. 26), Breen argues that the methodology of research into learning strategies is flawed for the following reasons:

   - There is no neat match between strategy and learning outcome.
   - Learner retrospection, diaries and so on are always shaped by the social relations in which they are embedded.

Go back and reread this critique. Do you agree with Breen?

3. How can research findings about the experiences of learners (such as Eva in Reading 1) be used to inform classroom practice?

Research

Writing a learning diary:
   You might ask a group of learners to do this, or start a diary yourself if you are currently learning a language.

Use the diary to reflect on what strategies you have been using; the social relations of the learning context that have had an impact on your learning; how you were feeling.

Try to find time to write this regularly, as soon as possible after the learning session (or make space for it at the end of each session).

Do this for a set period and then reread the entries.

- What insights into learning do they reveal?
- If possible, compare these insights with fellow learners to explore individual similarities and differences in learning experiences.

Additional reading

Peer, L. and Reid, G. (eds) (2000) *Multilingualism, Literacy and Dyslexia: A Challenge for Educators*, London: Fulton Publishers.

Roberts, C. (ed.) (2004) *Case Studies in ESOL Provision and Learners' Needs and Resources*, London: NRDC (see website for downloading details <www.nrdc.org.uk>).

Chapter 3

From mono- to multilingualism

Language use across settings and identities

Introduction

There is an unexplored assumption in much of SLA research that a learner has acquired one language from birth and, now that she is living in another country with a different language, she will gradually acquire this additional language and assimilate to 'native-speaker' norms. The two languages are seen as separate and stable entities. However, many people live in situations where two or more languages are in daily use and many of the world's urban settings, including British cities, may be called 'polyphonic': sites in which many languages are seen and heard. Studies have shown that people move between these languages in complex ways. In this chapter we focus on studies of linguistic diversity and pluralism, and explore the linguistic changes that result from the frequent contact of different languages in order to reconsider assumptions about language learners, and language use, in SLA research. We go on to discuss the relationships between language use and social identity, and the rationale of bilingual language programmes that address identity issues.

Being bilingual

The coexistence of two 'official' languages in a region or country is a common phenomenon in the world, resulting in a large number of bilingual speakers, and an established tradition of research into the acquisition and use of two languages (see e.g. Romaine, 1989). There can be no single definition of a bilingual, as the relations and uses of two languages in any area arise from particular historical and social factors. Some bilingual speakers have acquired the two languages simultaneously from an early age; some have added the second language later. The label of *bilingual* covers a variety of knowledge and use of two languages.

Code-switching

Socio-linguistic studies of bilingual speech communities have shown that it is common practice for bilingual speakers, when talking together, to use both languages to communicate. Speakers may embed one word or phrase from language B into an utterance in language A, or they may bring in a whole utterance in language B while mainly using language A, or alternate some conversational sequences in both languages. This phenomenon is known as code-switching. Examples of the uses of code-switching include comments as asides, to include/exclude/marginalize co-participants, to change the topic of conversation, and for puns and language play. However, linguists also stress the point that speakers draw on code-switching in multiple, creative ways, and that this linguistic mixing is fluid and changeable.

Before a systematic study of code-switching was carried out, it was often assumed that switching from one language to another was a sign of incompetence on the part of the speaker; that they did not have enough knowledge of one of the languages to communicate fully with it. Studies of bilingual language use in a variety of different parts of the world have since established that code-switching by competent bilingual speakers is a way of making meaning by drawing on two languages and an indication of bilingual ability.

From bilingualism to multilingualism

Code-switching is not limited to speakers of two languages, as studies of language use in multilingual communities have shown. In 1984, for example, Ben Rampton studied the language use of a multiracial adolescent peer group in the South Midlands of England, made up of youths of Indian, Pakistani, Caribbean and Anglo descent (Rampton, 1991). What he found was that there was a great deal of switching between languages and that some of this code-switching showed that informal language learning was going on within the groups. Youths of Anglo descent would mix Panjabi and Creole into English utterances, for example. He argued that the code-switching of these youths was used both to comment on social relations and as markers of social identity:

> Varieties [of language] are intricately associated with different social groups, ideologies, and settings, and speakers may either talk directly from within the social category associated with the language they are using, or . . . may set themselves up in dialogue against it, converging or diverging, being controlled by or controlling its socio-ideological connotations.
>
> (Rampton, 1991, p. 239)

An illustration of this self-conscious code-switching is Rampton's finding that fluent Panjabi/English bilingual teenagers would at times switch into what Rampton called 'ESL'. Presumably this was the kind of English (interlanguage) often spoken by Asian learners of English, containing deviant structures. He argued that their use of such language was ironic and that the youths did it to undermine or embarrass white authority figures. They were not only switching language, they were playing with different stereotyped identities. For Rampton, code-switching in this particular multilingual urban setting is part of the way that the speakers negotiate social boundaries.

Research shows that code-switching and language mixing are normal features of multilingual interactions and are shaped by both the social contexts and relations lived by the speakers, and their individual senses of self (see e.g. Martin-Jones (2000) for case studies of two Gujarati-speaking women in the UK). Speakers use their knowledge of different languages for meaning-making and to mark identity.

📖 Activity: Guided Reading

Reading 1:

Saxena, M. (1994) 'Literacies among the Panjabis in Southall (Britain)', section 1, in M. Hamilton, R. Barton and R. Ivanic (eds) *Worlds of Literacy*. Clevedon: Multilingual Matters, pp. 195–200.

You may wish to look at Reading 1 now, as Mukul Saxena's study of one family in Southall near the end of the twentieth century illustrates this linguistic behaviour by describing how multilingual individuals move through different languages and writing scripts. Since his focus was on the written language use of this family, their oral languages and code-switching are not recorded, but the mix of languages in their spoken interactions can be imagined.

How is the language use recorded in this study connected to religious and political identities?

This chapter is based on an ethnographic study of the literacy situation that exists among Panjabis, particularly Panjabi Hindus, in Southall, an area of the Borough of Ealing, in the western part of Greater London. The total population of Southall is about 120,000. The South Asian population of Southall is approximately 69,000. Of the total South Asian population, about 77% are Panjabi Sikhs, 20% are Panjabi Hindus, and the rest are a mix of various other South Asian minorities, including Panjabi, Gujarati and Urdu speaking Muslims, and Gujarati and Tamil speaking Hindus. Since Sikh and Hindu Panjabis are in the numerical majority, one is more likely to encounter the use of spoken and written Panjabi, Hindi and Urdu in Southall than that of Gujarati, Bengali or Tamil.

The literacy practices in the Panjabi community in Southall, West London, have changed enormously since the first group of Panjabi men came to Britain in 1950s. The third generation Panjabis are now living and growing up in a much more varied and complex situation of multilingual literacies than the first and second generation Panjabis ever did.

In the first part of this chapter I present a case study of a Panjabi Hindu family. It shows how individual members of this family are exposed to and make use of different literacies in Southall. It also draws attention to the values they assign to these literacies. In the second part, I provide an historical account of the literacy situation in the regions of origin of Panjabis. It will be helpful in understanding their current literacy practices in Southall. In the third and final part, I look at the political, economic, social and religious processes that have shaped the multiliteracy situation in Southall since the Panjabis migrated to Britain.

Multiliteracy practices in Southall: a case study of a Panjabi Hindu family

This section provides an account of some of the literacy practices of individual members of a Panjabi Hindu family in Southall. It will provide examples of how they make use of different literacies in their daily lives and, hopefully, throw some light on the literacy repertoire and literacy practices of the Panjabi Hindu community and the larger Panjabi community in Southall. We shall see, in this section, how individuals in this community are exposed to different print media; how they make literacy choices for different purposes; and how they value different literacies in their repertoire.

This family consists of a 4-year-old boy, his parents and grandparents. I chose this family because its members are fairly representative of the Panjabi Hindu community in Southall. They are brought up and have lived in different cultural and linguistic environments in India, East Africa and Britain. They are of different age groups and sex; they have had their education in different political, religious and cultural climates; and they have different attitudes towards different languages and orthographies.

SCRIPT CHOICES AND RELIGIOUS IDENTITIES

Panjabi is normally written in Gurmukhi script and associated with Sikhs.

ਨਸਲੀ ਭੇਦਭਾਵ ਦੇ ਵਿਰੁੱਧ ਸਾਲ ਦੀ ਪਾਲਿਸੀ ਦਾ ਵਿਸਥਾਰ

Hindi is normally written in Devanagari script and associated with Hindus.

नस्ली भेदभाव के विरुद्ध वर्ष की नीति के बारे में बयान

Urdu is normally written in Perso-Arabic script and associated with Muslims.

نسلی منافرت کے خلاف سال ـ پالیسی کا بیان

All three languages can be written in all three scripts. Everyday spoken Hindi and Urdu are very similar, especially in their grammatical structures. However, in certain contexts, users of these languages try to bring in the words of Sanskrit or Perso-Arabic origin in their speech and writing to show their allegiance to Hindus or Muslims.

This is one of the families in Southall with whom I have spent most time. Over the course of five years, I stayed with them on many occasions and observed their literacy practices. Initially, my visits to and stays with this family were a matter of hospitality extended to a student from their country of origin having the same linguistic background. However, over the period, the acquaintance gradually grew into a close relationship. As I was accepted and treated as a member of the family, I could participate in their day-to-day activities. This relationship also provided me with the freedom of questioning and discussing their actions and views, even though they were fully aware of my study and its purpose.

The literacy events presented below all took place but did not necessarily happen in one single day. In order to give the account more cohesion they are presented as if they occurred in a single day.

Grandfather (educated in the Panjab in pre-liberated India; migrated to East Africa before coming to England)

He takes bus no. 74 signposted in English 'Greenford' to go to the Community Club for the elderly people. There he reads a local newspaper in Urdu about the South Asians in Britain, Southall's local news, and political news from India and Pakistan. He picks up a national newspaper in English, skims through it to get general news about British and international affairs.

He then walks down a few blocks to a publishing house which publishes a fortnightly newspaper to promote Panjabi nationalism in terms of its secular political ideology and Panjabi culture. He exchanges greetings with the editor in Panjabi and shows him a poem he has written in Panjabi/Gurmukhi in praise of Panjab rivers. The editor considers it for publication.

On the way home, he goes to a book store which specialises in print media (newspaper, magazine, children's and literary books, novels, etc.) from India, Pakistan and Britain in various South Asian scripts. He buys a Hindi film magazine from India for his daughter-in-law. He also notices advertising posters in English in the street.

At home, when his grandson comes back from school, he reads him a nursery book written in English.

Grandmother (brought up in East Africa with little formal education: learnt Hindi at home)

She waits for a bus, at the bus stop, to go to a Hindu temple. She does not read English. One of the buses that go to the temple is No. 36. When buses other than No. 36 come, she checks with the drivers (bus drivers in Southall are mostly Panjabi) if the buses go in the direction of the temple. None does. No. 36 arrives with Hayes sign written in English. Though she does not read English, she recognises the shape of the word, because she sees it often. She also recognises the driver and the adverts on the bus. She boards the bus without feeling a need to check it with the driver.

She compensates her lack of knowledge of written English by relying on her memory of certain objects, events, people, etc., and assistance from other people.

On entering the temple, she reads a notice in Hindi about the weekend's events at the temple. Inside the main hall, after offering prayers to each of the Hindi gods, she asks the priest about the date of a particular festival. The priest then checks a yearly magazine from the Panjab, written in Perso-Arabic script, about the Hindu religious calendar. Later, with other women and some elderly men, she listens to a Hindu religious book read out in Hindi by the priest. Then she goes upstairs where there is a Hindu cultural centre and a library. She reads a Hindi newspaper from India there, and borrows a religious book in Hindi.

On the way home, she notices shop names displayed in bilingual signs in Panjabi-English, Hindi-English or Urdu-English. She goes into a *sari* (an Indian women's dress) shop. The shop has a English-Hindi bilingual sign outside. The shop owner is the president of the Hindi temple.

Father (born in East Africa, but brought up and educated in England from an early age).

In the morning, he reads an English newspaper for national and international news before leaving for work. At work, he supervises about 250 workers of South Asian origin in a factory. As and when required, he also mediates, as an interpreter, between the workers and the factory bosses. He also has the responsibility of making available bilingual materials published by social service agencies on safety, workers' legal rights, medical benefits etc. in the factory.

After work, in the evening, he goes to a Hindu temple where he is a member of the temple executive committee. With other committee members, he prepares a draft letter in English about the annual general meeting to be sent out to the registered members of the temple. It was agreed that when the temple has enough funds, the committee will send English-Hindi bilingual letters and notices to its members, as one of the roles of the temple is to promote Hindi. At the moment, the temple has only an English typewriter. The committee members also prepare some hand-written notices in Hindi for the temple notice board regarding the agenda of the annual general meeting.

On the way home, he notices some new Sikh nationalistic and communal slogans on street walls written in Panjabi. He discusses these slogans with his family when he comes home. At home, his mother reads to him from a weekly Hindi newspaper published locally about some local news an some news from the Panjab. This newspaper also has a few articles on Indian Hindi films written in English which he reads himself.

Mother (born, brought up and educated in the Panjab during and after reorganisation period of the Panjab in India before coming to England for marriage).

In the morning, she takes her son to a nearby nursery. She brings back a note in English from the teacher about some activity which the child and the parents have contributed to. She shows it to her husband in the evening. He reads it and explains it to her in Panjabi.

After finishing the household chores, she gets a little time to read a few pages from a Hindi novel. Later, with her mother-in-law, she writes a letter to a relative in Delhi. They discuss and write the contents of the letter in Panjabi-Hindi mixed code using Devanagari script. She also writes a letter in Panjabi-Gurmukhi to a friend in the Panjab.

In the evening, before putting her son to sleep, she tells him a story in Panjabi.

Son (born in Southall)

In the morning as he enters the school, he sees bilingual signs. He can distinguish between Gurmukhi, Devanagari and Roman scripts. In the classroom, he is exposed only to the Roman script for teaching and learning purposes.

At home in the afternoon, his grandmother sends him with a small shopping list in Hindi/Devanagari to a corner shop next door. The shopkeeper records the goods sold to the boy in Hindi/Devanagari in his ledger.

During the day, the boy observes his parents and grandparents using different literacies for different purposes.

Dinner time

One of the topics discussed during and after dinner is why the child should learn Hindi or Panjabi. The grandfather wants his grandson to learn Panjabi in the Gurmukhi script when he goes to school, but not in the Sikh temple. He thinks this way his grandson can learn Panjabi and retain Panjabi culture. He favours Panjabi because it is also the official language of the Panjab state. However, grandmother, mother and father think that the child should learn Hindi/Devanagari. Grandmother and father take more of a religious stance whereas mother takes the nationalistic/ secular stance. Grandmother and father think that it is important to learn Hindi to retain Hindu culture and religion; whereas mother thinks that the child should learn Hindi because it is the national language of India. A further argument put forward in favour of Hindi related to the interpersonal communicative functions of literacy: grandmother, mother and father argue in favour of Hindi by saying that with the knowledge of the Hindi script the child will be able to correspond with the relatives both in Delhi and the Panjab, whereas the knowledge of the written Panjab would restrict him only to the Panjab. Grandfather is outvoted, and it is decided that the child would go to the Hindi voluntary classes held in the Hindu temple initially and later would also opt for Hindi in school.

In the above section, I have talked about what individual members of this family do with different literacies in different situations, and how they value these literacies. In the following two sections, I will address the questions: why do these people make different literacy choices in their everyday lives the way they do, and how are these choices shaped in different social conditions in which they are living or have lived? These questions will help us understand that the multiple literacy choices Panjabi individuals of Southall make in their everyday literacy practices reflect their differing ideological way of thinking. Nevertheless, rather than restraining their actions, these choices provide them with multiple identities and freedom to operate in different worlds of literacies to achieve different goals. These questions will also reveal the fact that a decade or so ago one would not have encountered this kind of multiplicity of literacies in Southall as reflected by their literacy practices.

Saxena goes on to give a historical account of language use and change in the Panjab (not included in this reading) which describes a multilingual society where movement between different languages and scripts is the norm. He summarizes these changes as follows:

> In response to the domination of Muslim religion and their Urdu language and Perso-Arabic script in the Panjab, there was a growth of Hindu and Sikh religious revival movements and the literature associated with them at the turn of this century. In consequence, Sikhs came to attach increasing significance to the writing of Panjabi in the Gurmukhi script as the language of the Sikhs and of the Sikh religion just as Hindus developed an attachment to Hindi in the Devanagari script. Close symbolic linkages, therefore, were made between Panjabi, Hindi and Urdu with Gurmukhi, Devanagari and Perso-Arabic scripts for religious reasons.
>
> (Saxena, 1994, p. 202)

As we can see from this summary and his case study of the different generations of one family now living in the UK, the spoken and written languages that an individual will learn in her life result from a complex set of factors including religious affiliation, education and political changes.

From English to Englishes: questioning monolingualism

In her analysis of bilingual and biliteracy studies, Nancy Hornberger makes the point that code-switching is not unique to bi- and multilingual communities. She argues that monolingualism and bilingualism are more alike than different because monolinguals are not limited to one way of speaking only. Where bi- and multilingual speakers switch languages, monolingual speakers switch between regional and standardized varieties (Hornberger, 1994, p. 115). We also switch from one discourse to another as we move between settings. My discussions with research colleagues usually involve a lot of academic discourse, but my way of talking and the language I use changes when I am in the local park with my dogs chatting to other dog walkers. Hornberger describes monolingualism and bilingualism, not as polar opposites, but as 'theoretical endpoints on what is in reality a continuum of features' (p. 105). Monolingual speakers draw on their knowledge of the diversity within one language to negotiate social boundaries and make meanings.

As a language moves from one country to another this diversity increases. The spread of English around the world has brought it into regular contact with many different languages, and in many different contexts. This contact has resulted in change, and we now have different varieties of English and different 'Englishes' such as Indian English or Malay English. Thus we can add to some multilingual settings the speaking of different Englishes, as well as other languages.

Activity: Guided Reading

Reading 2:

Crystal, D. (2001) 'The future of Englishes', in A. Burns and C. Coffin (eds) *Analysing English in a Global Context: A Reader*, London, Routledge, pp. 54–55, 55–6, 59–61.

You may now wish to read the extract by David Crystal, which gives more detail on how English is changing in its contact with other languages. In this text Crystal seems mainly to be addressing those who teach English as a foreign language in other countries.

Is his argument, that standard English is losing its power, relevant for ESOL teachers and learners here?

The changing situation

English is now spoken by more people (as a first, second, or foreign language) than any other language and is recognized by more countries as a desirable lingua franca than any other language. This is not the place to recapitulate the relevant statistics, insofar as they can be established: this information is available elsewhere (for my own estimates, see Crystal, 1995, 1997; see also Graddol, 1997). But it is important to recognize that the unprecedented scale of the growth in usage (approaching a quarter of the world's population) has resulted in an unprecedented growth in regional varieties.

Variation, of course, has always been part of the language, given that Angles, Saxons, and Jutes must have spoken different Germanic dialects. The emergence of Scots can be traced back to the beginning of the Middle English period. In the eighteenth century, Noah Webster was one of many who argued the need to recognize a distinct American (as opposed to British) tongue. And the issue of identity has been central to debate about the nature of creole and pidgin Englishes around the world. But it is only in recent decades (chiefly, since the independence era of the 1960s) that the diversity has become so dramatic, generating a huge literature on 'world Englishes' and raising the question of linguistic identity in fresh and intriguing ways.

The chief aim of McArthur's book *The English Language* (1998) is to draw attention to the remarkable 'messiness' which characterizes the current world English situation, especially in second-language contexts. Typically, a 'new English' is not a homogeneous entity, with clear-cut boundaries, and an easily definable phonology, grammar, and lexicon. On the contrary, communities which are putting English to use are doing so in several different ways. As McArthur puts it (p. 2), 'stability and flux go side by side, centripetal and centrifugal forces operating at one and the same time.' And when actual examples of language in use are analysed, in such multilingual settings as Malaysia and Singapore, all kinds of unusual hybrids come to light.

Different degrees of language mixing are apparent: at one extreme, a sentence might be used which is indistinguishable from Standard English. At the other extreme a sentence might use so many words and constructions from a contact language that it becomes unintelligible to those outside a particular community. In between, there are varying degrees of hybridization, ranging from the use of a single lexical borrowing within a sentence to several borrowings, and from the addition of a single borrowed syntactic construction (such as a tag question) to a reworking of an entire sentence structure. In addition, of course, the pronunciation shows similar degrees of variation, from a standard British or American accent to an accent which diverges widely from such standards both in segmental and nonsegmental (intonational, rhythmical) ways (Crystal, 1996).

For example, within a few lines from less than half-a-minute of Malaysian conversation, we can extract the following utterances (for the original conversation, see Baskaran, 1994). At the top of the list is a sentence which could be called Standard Colloquial English; below it are other sentences which show increasing degrees of departure from this norm, grammatically and lexically. At the bottom is a sentence (in this English dialogue) which is entirely Colloquial Malay.

Standard colloquial English
Might as well go window-shopping a bit, at least.

Grammatical hybrids
My case going to be adjourned anyway.
   [auxiliary verb omitted]
Okay, okay, at about twelve, can or not?
   [distinctive tag question in English]

You were saying you wanted to go shopping,
   nak perga tak? [addition and tag question in Malay 'Want to go, not?']
Can lah, no problem one! ['I can'; *lah* is an emphatic particle)

Lexical hybrids
No chance to ronda otherwise. [Malay 'loaf']
You were saying, that day, you wanted to beli some barang-barang. [Malay 'buy
   . . . things']
But if anything to do with their stuff – golf or snooker or whatever, then dia
   pun boleh sabar one. [Malay 'he too can be patient']

Colloquial Malay
Betul juga. ['True also']

Continua of this kind have long been recognized in creole language studies. What
is novel, as McArthur points out, is the way phenomena of this kind have become
so widespread, happening simultaneously in communities all over the world. After
reviewing several speech situations, he concludes (p. 22):

> Worldwide communication centres on Standard English, which however
> radiates out into many kinds of English and many other languages, producing
> clarity here, confusion there, and novelties and nonsenses everywhere. The
> result can be – often is – chaotic, but despite the blurred edges, this latter-day
> Babel manages to work.

. . .

Hybridization has been a feature of English since Anglo-Saxon times. Any history of
English shows that the language has always been something of a 'vacuum-cleaner',
sucking in words and expressions from the other languages with which it has come
into contact. . . . But today, with more contact being made with other languages than
ever before, the scale of the borrowing is much greater than it has been in the past.
A wider range of languages is involved: there are over 350 modern languages listed
in the etymology files of the *Oxford English Dictionary*. And the borrowing is now
found in all varieties of English, and not just in the more academic or professional
domains.

. . .

Part 2 Teaching matters

Much of the evidence presented in this paper is anecdotal. It can do little more than
provide motivation for hypotheses. There is a real need for empirical research into

these hybrid language situations. But it is plain that the emergence of hybrid trends and varieties raises all kinds of theoretical and pedagogical questions:

- They blur the long-standing distinctions between 'first', 'second' and 'foreign' language.
- They make us reconsider the notion of 'standard', especially when we find such hybrids being used confidently and fluently by groups of people who have education and influence in their own regional setting.
- They present the traditionally clear-cut notion of 'translation' with all kinds of fresh problems, for (to go back to the Malaysian example) at what point in a conversation should we say that a notion of translation is relevant, as we move from 'understanding' to 'understanding most of the utterance precisely' to 'understanding little of the utterance precisely ("getting the drift" or "gist")' to 'understanding none of the utterance, despite its containing several features of English'?
- And, to move into the sociolinguistic dimension, hybrids give us new challenges in relation to language attitudes: for example, at what point our insistence on the need for translation cause an adverse reaction from the participants, who might maintain they are 'speaking English', even though we cannot understand them?

Towards a new pedagogy

'O brave new world, That has such people in't.' Miranda's exclamation (from *The Tempest*, V. i. 88) is apposite. It is a brave new world, indeed; and those who have to be bravest of all are the teachers of English. I am never sure whether to call language teaching or translating the most difficult of all the language tasks; both are undeniably highly demanding and professional activities (and it is one of the world's greatest scandals that such professions can be so badly paid). But in a world where traditional models and values are changing so rapidly, the task facing the teacher, in particular, is immense. Keeping abreast of all that is taking place is a nightmare in itself. Deciding what to teach, given the proliferation of new and competing models, requires metaphors which go beyond nightmares. Is there any consensus emerging about what a teacher should do in such circumstances?

My impression, as I travel around and listen to people reporting on their experiences, is that this situation – one of rapid linguistic transition – is demanding an increased recognition of the fundamental importance of distinguishing between production and reception skills in language teaching.

From a production point of view, there is a strong case for pedagogical con-servatism. If one is used to teaching Standard English and an RP (received pronunciation) accent, this argument goes, then one should continue to do so, for a whole range of familiar reasons – the linguistic knowledge base is there in the various analyses and descriptions, there are copious course-books and materials, and there is a well-understood correspondence between the norms of spoken and written expression (important for examination purposes as well as for reading literature). In short, there is a general familiarity with this variety which must breed a modicum of content.

But from the viewpoint of listening comprehension, there is an equally strong case for pedagogical innovation. It is a fact that RP is changing (to be precise, continuing to change), and that many forms of 'regionally modified RP' are now to be heard among educated people in Britain and abroad. It is a fact that several regional accents (e.g. Edinburgh Scots, Yorkshire) are now more prestigious than they used to be, and are being used in settings which would have been inconceivable twenty years ago – such as by presenters on radio and television, or by switchboard operators in the rapidly growing domain of telemarketing. . . . It is a fact that new regional first-language standards, in dialect as well as accent, are emerging in such countries as Australia and South Africa.

It is a fact that new regional second-language standards are emerging in such areas as West Africa and the subcontinent of India though less obvious how far these are country-restricted: see Crystal (1995: 358ff.). And it is a fact that there are new hybrids emerging in foreign-language contexts all over the English-speaking world.

Flexibility and variety

If this is the case, teachers need to prepare their students for a world of staggering linguistic diversity. Somehow, they need to expose them to as many varieties of English as possible, especially those which they are most likely to encounter in their own locale. And above all, teachers need to develop a truly flexible attitude towards principles of usage. The absolutist concept of 'proper English' or 'correct English', which is so widespread, needs to be replaced by relativistic models in which literary and educated norms are seen to maintain their place alongside other norms, some of which depart radically from what was once recognized as 'correct'.

Yes, familiarity breeds content – but also contempt, when it fails to keep pace with social realities. All over the world there are people losing patience with what they perceive to be an irrational traditionalism. You will all have your own stories of the uncertainties and embarrassments generated when accepted local usages come into conflict with traditional standards. While there are still some parts of the world where there is a reverential attitude towards British English in general, and RP in particular, this attitude is rapidly being replaced by a dynamic pragmatism. if people in a country increasingly observe their own high-ranking, highly educated people using hybrid forms, if they increasingly hear linguistic diversity on the World Service of the BBC and other channels, if they find themselves being taught by mother-tongue speakers who themselves reflect current trends in their regionally tinged speech, then who can blame them if they be to be critical of teaching perspectives which reflect nothing but a parochial past?

The new reality

. . .

The emphasis has got to move away from 'British English' or, at least, to a revised concept of British English which has variety at the core. For what is British English today? The spoken British English of Britain is already a mass of hybrid forms, with Celtic and immigrant language backgrounds a major presence. Accent variation is always the clearest index diversity, because it is a symbol of identity: What we might call 'classical' RP (as described by Gimson et al.) is probably down to about 2 per cent of the population now; and modified forms of RP are increasingly the norm, and regional accents, as we have seen, are increasingly accepted in educated contexts which would have rejected them a generation ago.

If you want to hear good classical RP spoken by whole communities, you will more likely find it in Moscow or Copenhagen than in Manchester or Reading. In Britain itself, diversity is the reality. 'Real Britannia: What Does it Mean to be British?' shouts a headline in the *Independent* earlier this week, and the author Suzanne Moore comments, towards the end of a piece in which 'a nation in search of an identity' is the theme:

> The question, then, is how do we create a modern version of Britishness that is inclusive rather than exclusive, that is based in the present rather than in the past, that is urban rather than rural, that is genuinely multicultural, that does not reside in 'middle England' but amongst a society of hybrids and mongrels.

Linguistic diversity and language health

Our linguistic past has been shaped by recognizing the value of linguistic diversity; and I believe the same should be true for our linguistic future. ELT policy-making, accordingly, should make diversity its central principle – removing it from the periphery to which it has hitherto largely been assigned. No country has dared do this yet. . . . But to do so may make many feel uncomfortable. . . .

Even a statement recognizing the value of competing linguistic standards is too much for some. I was a member of the panel which discussed English language issues at the British Council's launch of David Graddol's book *The Future of English?* (1997), and I hinted at this view in a contribution I made there. Afterwards, at the buffet, someone came up and asked me if my notion of linguistic tolerance of English diversity extended to such things as the errors foreigners made. I said it all depended on what you mean by an error. *I am knowing*, for example, is not allowed in traditional Standard English, but it is normal in some parts of the world, such as the Indian subcontinent (and also, incidentally, in some British dialects). Would you correct a Frenchman who said *I am knowing*, then, he asked? It all depends, I said. Not if he was learning Indian English. My interlocutor's face told me that the concept of a Frenchman wanting to learn Indian English was, at the very least, novel.

There was a pause. Then he said, 'Are you saying that, in the British Council, we should be letting our teachers teach Indian English, and not British English?'

'If the occasion warranted it, yes,' I said.

'I don't like the sound of that,' he said, and he literally fled from me, upsetting a glass of wine in the process. He didn't hear me add: 'Or even other languages.'

For in some parts of the world, the wisest advice would be to recommend that we divert some of our resources to maintaining the life of minority languages. Identity and intelligibility are both needed for a healthy linguistic life. And the responsibility of doing something to try to minimize the ongoing damage to the world's ecolinguistic environment – with a language dying somewhere in the world, on average, every fortnight or so – belongs to everyone, whether they are ELT specialists or not.

Crystal mainly discusses varieties of English used in countries with other official languages. There are, however, established varieties of English spoken within English-speaking countries. Two examples of these are Jamaican Creole in the Caribbean and the UK, and Black Vernacular English in the USA. Both of these varieties used to be considered as limited, substandard dialects, and speakers were stigmatized outside their communities. Studies of these varieties (see e.g. ILEA, 1990) have critiqued these negative views. They argue that awareness of the differences between varieties of English and standard English should be part of school curricula (see Davis *et al.*, (1997) for discussions on Australian and American varieties; also Richardson, 2002).

What is the relevance of these studies to the ESOL classroom?

Knowledge about language use in bi- and multilingual settings can add to our understanding about language learners in our classrooms. Switching between languages is, of course, also a feature of language classroom interaction, as learners struggle to express themselves in the new language. This form of code-switching, however, is a learning strategy for language students, and so has a different function from switches made in bilingual talk, where both speaker and listener share linguistic and cultural knowledge. While language mixing may not be a problem in the language classroom, learners who are accustomed to multilingual talk may have some problems with communication in monolingual workplaces and educational environments. Curricula and accreditation rarely acknowledge multilingual ways of meaning-making (see Bhatt and Martin-Jones (1992) for a critique of school policies and materials).

On the other hand, an individual who arrives in the UK with a different variety of English may have a harder time in education than someone who speaks one or two languages that have an established history and international recognition. A language profile of a young Nigerian woman, Victoria, illustrates this (Savitzky, 1986). Victoria's first languages were Ibo and English, but when her family moved to Lagos education was given in Yoruba. She was also taught to read and write in English in both primary and secondary school. In addition, she used Pidgin with her neighbours, and Hausa in the market. When she came to England she could communicate fluently in spoken English but had a lot of problems with examinations due to differences between the standard written English of our education system and the variety of English taught in Nigeria. Research has also shown that misunderstandings in spoken communication can arise from differences between standard English and other varieties' intonation and stress patterns (see Cameron, 2001, ch. 8).

Language and identity

What studies of bilingual and multilingual communities also highlight is that language is not only a medium for communication, it is also a symbol of social identity, and thus can become a site of tension both within individuals trying to work out their own complex set of identities, and between groups of individuals. Consideration of relations between language use and social identity are not included in most SLA studies. Rampton critiques research into language-learning processes for having a narrow view of language which ignores its multiple nature and its social identification function (Rampton, 1991, p. 241). He argues, for example, that the term 'native speaker', frequently used in writings about SLA no longer applies and should be replaced by the term 'expert speaker'. Rampton draws on a social theory of literacy in his critique and argues that much of SLA research is based on an autonomous model of language learning and use and this is reflected in its terminology (see Barton (1994); Street (1984) for explanations of the autonomous model). So, how do educators tap into the potentially rich linguistic resources of ESOL learners?

Bilingual education

Recognition of the relationships between language use and identity has led to the development of a variety of bilingual language programmes. Many of these have been set up in the USA where there are large populations of migrants who share a common language. These programmes tend to focus on literacy tuition in their home language as well as in English, so will be discussed in the next chapter on learning the written language. Here, we will consider the 'El Barrio Popular' Education Program, a community-based adult programme in New York, because it emphasizes the role of oral language in the bilingual language-learning process, as well as the written language (Rivera, 1999). It is a programme that aims to provide literacy and basic education in both Spanish and English to the mainly unemployed women in the community it serves. Rivera argues that including Spanish in the process both lessens language and cultural shock, and taps into the multiple sources of knowledge within the families and communities. The curriculum is based on research units in which participants choose topics to investigate within their communities. The results of the research are then used to create videos which are shown on public-access television. These videos may be made in Spanish or English, thus providing opportunities for the students to develop their oral abilities in either language.

To reinforce the equal status of the two languages in the programme, most of the language teachers are bilingual themselves, and students and graduate students are also trained to work in the programme as 'popular teachers'. By 1995 almost half of the staff came from the same community as the learners, and had been students there themselves.

Bringing the learners' first languages into what is expected to be an ESOL classroom means spending energy and resources on a language that is not usually designated as an official medium of communication of a country or region. Such a pedagogy thus often attracts criticism which is not based on educational principles, but comes from anxieties over national identity. Governments are often reluctant to provide funds for such programmes. Rivera describes the search for funding for the El Barrio Program as a constant struggle. Joseph Lo Bianco, in a critique of American government policy, explains why bilingual programmes seem threatening:

> Mastery of foreign languages, spoken far away 'in other countries', is something sufficiently divorced from daily life that it can be appreciated as a skill. Its mastery is likely to be less than the mastery and attachment to English, not thereby challenging presumed deep attachments of national allegiance. However, when the languages are less foreign, when emotional attachment and mastery may be high, their study, public use and maintenance 'threatens civilisation'. No longer a skill, but sedition.
>
> (Lo Bianco, 2000, p. 99)

There have also been bilingual programmes in the UK, and one focusing on literacy in Sheffield is discussed in Chapter 4. But most ESOL policy and accreditation remains firmly monolingual (see e.g. Hamilton, 1996; Roberts, 2003).

The El Barrio Program, and other bilingual programmes in the USA, have also tried to break down classroom walls by adopting a participatory approach as a methodology, and bilingual education is imparted within a critical approach which explicitly requires learners to connect their individual experiences to larger, oppressive social patterns (see also Reading 3 in Chapter 4 for an explanation of this approach). The learners are encouraged to participate in all curriculum decision-making, and to research topics they consider to have an impact upon their lives and those of their families. Rivera argues that making the videos becomes a transformative tool for the learners: 'The women who made the videos were no longer students learning to read and write and to speak English or exploited and displaced workers of the garment industry; they became informants on their own experience, researchers and video producers' (Rivera, 1999, p. 493). Such an approach provides one solution to Rampton's critique of the positioning of the language 'learner' as a-cultural and de-racinated.

This approach overtly embraces the ideological message that is inherent in bilingual language programmes for minority ethnic adults living in a different culture and learning its dominant language. Given the interweaving of language use with individual and national identity, it is, perhaps, impossible to ignore the fact that additional language education is both a political and a personal issue.

Multilingual practices in the classroom

Bilingual programmes inevitably can only take place where there are sufficient populations of language speakers. Many ESOL classes are in themselves small multilingual worlds bringing together speakers of many different languages. One such class is the subject of the final reading of this chapter.

Activity: Guided Reading

Reading 3:

McLaughlin, J. (1986) 'Developing writing in English from mother-tongue story-telling'. *Language Issues*, 1: 31–34.

Reading 3 shows one way in which an ESOL tutor in Britain brings the many languages, and cultures, of her students into the learning process.

How else can a teacher, who may be monolingual, encourage multilingual practices in the ESOL classroom?

The work which I will describe was done with a class in the south of the London Borough of Lewisham: in that area the two main language groups are Cantonese speakers from Vietnam and Turkish Cypriots. Both groups were represented in the class, which met in the evening twice a week; there were also a young woman from Italy, another from Cyprus who spoke Greek, and a woman from Norway working in a nearby college. It was a mixed-level class; the level of spoken English ranged from elementary to low intermediate.

Most of the students enjoyed doing written exercises and were making good progress in functional writing and structured written work; one or two were able to write quite well but were diffident about doing so. One woman needed basic literacy and did separate work with a volunteer during these parts of the class. In general, I felt the students lacked the confidence to develop fluency in writing and would benefit from some work which would encourage freedom of expression and imagination.

For this reason I had for some time wanted to encourage the telling and writing of folk tales with this group, but had not so far succeeded in doing so. Mostly my suggestions had received the reply that they 'didn't know any'.

Why choose storytelling as an activity? As in most decisions about teaching, there was a general principle and a particular application to this group. In general I have found the telling of folk tales and traditional stories in class has been an activity much enjoyed and valued by the students, that it liberated resources of language that might not otherwise have been tapped, and that it contributed to the cohesion and cooperation of the group by stimulating interest in other cultures and traditions. This last was for me a particularly important consideration with this class: the Cantonese speakers were a group of men who all knew each other well; the other students were women who, with the exception of two, did not have any contact outside the class. The students from Vietnam remained a cohesive and self-supporting group; while the atmosphere in the class was generally pleasant, there was little contact between them and the others. I also wanted to produce some texts which would have a dual purpose: to provide some reading material which would be relevant and interesting, and to increase the confidence of the students in their ability to write in English by seeing their own work used as teaching materials. (For a fuller account of the reasons why I believe creative writing, in which I include the writing of traditional stories, is important in ESL, see my article 'Creative Writing in English as a Second Language Work' in *Viewpoints* No 3.)

It was here that the use of the mother tongue came in. I should perhaps make some comment here on the use of languages other than English in the classes that I teach: while I cannot claim to have done much in the way of bilingual materials, mainly because of the multilingual nature of the classes, it is accepted practice in the classes that I teach that students use their own languages whenever and however they wish. The theoretical and practical reasons for the use of other languages in the classroom have been considered elsewhere, notably in *ESL Issues 1: Mother Tongue and ESL*. For me the two main reasons have always been that the use of their own languages by the students means that they can use a wide range of learning strategies which are not available to them in the medium of English, and is therefore simply sound educational practice, and that the constant presence of other languages in the classroom prevents the culturally and linguistically intimidating effect of imposed monolingualism. This is why, in the tape-script reproduced in this article, the words 'Tell it to Figen' are intended and understood to be a suggestion that the student tells the story in Turkish to her friend. No other negotiation was necessary, as the two people in question were quite used to working in this way.

The telling of the stories came about in the following way. One evening I produced a bundle of different things – magazines, readers, newspaper cuttings and so on – and asked the students to choose something that interested them, in the hope that this would produce some ideas for discussion and writing. One of the Turkish-speaking women picked up one of the Nasreddin stories (from the materials pack produced by Erica Buckmaster for the RSA Diploma) and said that she knew lots of stories about him. She hadn't realised that *that* was the kind of thing I was talking about when I asked them to tell stories. This shows how students can undervalue their own traditions and cultures in the context of learning English. This was Figen, the interpreter on the tape. This particular session took place towards the end of the evening class when the students had already done quite a lot of work and were in a relaxed frame of mind.

In the first part of the tape which I made of this session, Figen talks about Nasreddin Hoca, describing his character and abilities, and gives some examples of his cleverness. There are also some contributions in Turkish and English by Figen's friend and cousin, Shoray. The tapescript reproduced here starts at a point where Shoray clearly wished to say more, but could not do so in English.

Figen:	Nasreddin Hoca* is really a man.
Jane:	He's a. . . . ?
Figen:	Really . . . and he died . . . Aksehir . . .
Jane:	Ah . . . he was a real man.
Figen:	Yes.
Jane:	When?
Figen:	Long time ago (*Shoray: Yes*) Yes.
Jane:	And where did he live?
Figen:	Turkey . . . Aksehir.
Shoray:	Aksehir.
Jane:	Do you know more about him, Shoray?
Shoray:	I know . . .
Jane:	Can't you . . . all right, tell it, tell it to Figen.
Shoray:	(*speaks Turkish*)
Jane:	Can you tell it, Figen?
Figen:	What do you call water . . . ?

* Pronunciation in English: hoja

Shoray:	Floor.
Jane:	Water?
Shoray:	Garden, garden, no house.
Jane:	A pond, when you have water in the garden?
Shoray:	Yes.
Figen:	Like a pond, but, you know . . .
Shoray:	Inside.
Jane:	In the house?
Figen:	No, garden.
Shoray:	Garden, yes.
Figen:	Like a pond, and you get water . . .
Jane:	Oh, you mean . . . for . . . to drink? A hole, the well, a well. When you put a bucket in (*Shoray: Yes!* and you bring the, yes . . . It's called a well.
Shoray:	(*speaks Turkish*)
Figen:	It was a night time, Nasreddin went to the . . .
Jane:	To the well (*writes on board*).
Shoray:	Yes! Well.
Figen:	To get some water (*Jane: Yes*). And he saw the moon.
Shoray:	Water, you know, moon, night.
Jane:	Yes. In the water.
Figen:	He thought he pulls (*Shoray: Out*) the moon, (*Jane: Yes*) and he pulls, and the rope . . .
Shoray:	(*speaks Turkish*)
Figen:	He said very heavy (*Jane: Yes*) and . . . he thought he pulls the moon . . .
Jane:	He thought he'd pulled the moon . . . out of the water . . .
Figen:	And pulled, and pulls, pulls and he . . .
Shoray:	(*speaks Turkish*) Broken.
Figen:	The rope.
Shoray:	(*speaks Turkish*)
Jane:	The rope broke.
Figen and Shoray:	Yes.
Figen:	He lays down.
Shoray:	. . . up, and after see . . . (*speaks Turkish*)
Jane:	So he fell over.
Figen:	Yes, he fell over; when he fells over, he lay down, and he saw the moon . . .
Shoray:	On the sky.
Figen:	In the sky . . . and he thought he pulled the moon out.

(*Laughter from class*)

Clearly some detailed language needs have been revealed by this work, but here we are concerned with the development of narrative storytelling. After a story has been told in this way there are various options open to the teacher and the class.

1. Each student can write a version of the same story – in their own language or in English. If necessary, some question-prompts can be given as a guide: Where did he go? What did he want? and so on.
2. The teacher can produce a transcript of the tape to be turned into a connected written narrative, either as a group or individual activity.
3. The teacher can produce a connected written narrative version for use as a reading text and for other activities.
4. The telling of the story orally can be used as a stimulus for writing other stories, perhaps concerning a similar character or theme.
5. The students could be asked to produce their own versions of the story at a later date. They could then discuss the differences between these versions.
6. It may be better to do nothing. They may have had enough storytelling for that day, and the activity may be regarded as sufficiently valuable in itself as fostering confidence, self-expression and the sharing of experience.

The Nasreddin stories were received with enthusiasm by the class. 'Very good story' was the verdict of the Vietnamese students on at least one occasion.

Why didn't *they* tell some stories, then? They said it was 'too difficult'. So I tried a method which was first suggested to me by Ruth Hamblin of Islington AEI, and which I have found extremely useful. The students told the story as a group. Acting as scribe, I wrote it down, read it back to the students to check the details, and brought it back the next week as a reading text. The students from Vietnam being a monolingual group, the story was told through discussion in the mother tongue. The story of 'The Monk of Saolin' reproduced here was the end product of some minutes of animated conversation in Cantonese, much of it clearly entertaining to those taking part. All the Cantonese speakers, even those most reticent in English, contributed, and the following text, with my help, was the work of all of them:

The Monk of Saolin

A long time ago there was an old man who lived in a temple. He was called the Monk of Saolin. He was a teacher, and what he taught was laziness. He taught his students how to be lazy.

There was a boy whose name was Kwan. He had a very rich father, but he was very lazy. He didn't want to learn anything. He heard that the Monk of Saolin was teaching students how to be lazy.

Kwan went to the temple, but the temple door was shut. The Monk of Saolin was inside the temple, teaching students how to be lazy.

The monk looked out and saw Kwan. He said: 'Why don't you come in?'

Kwan said: 'I'm waiting for the wind to blow the door open.'

The monk waited a long time, and then he went to open the door. He said, 'Come in.'

Kwan said: 'You must carry me on your back, then I'll come in.'

Then the monk said to Kwan: 'I can't teach you anything. You already know enough about how to be lazy.'

I tried another approach with Lucia, the young Italian woman; this time my contribution was possible because of my knowledge of Italian. Lucia insisted that she couldn't write anything in English, least of all a story. So I suggested that she should write a story in Italian, and I said I would translate it for her. The following bilingual text was the result.

Tra due litiganti il terzo gode

Un leone e un orso, avendo ucciso un capriolo, che avevano trovato in una selva, nel fare le parti vennero in discordia e cominciarono a corn battere tra loro. Gia erano tanto le ferite, che, stanchi del lungo combattimento e privi di forze giacevano in terra. Una volpe, che da lontano aveva tutto osservato, si accosto, e avendo rubata il capriolo, fuggi con questo. Il leone e l'orso videro cite la volpe aveva rapito il capriolo; ma non potendola inseguire, dissero 'Tra due litiganti il tero gode'.

When two quarrel, the third profits

A lion and a bear, having killed a deer which they had found in the forest, began to quarrel while they were dividing it up and a fight started. Their injuries were so bad that, tired by the fight and without any more strength, they lay down on the ground. A fox who had watched everything from a distance came near, and when she had stolen the deer, she ran away with it. The lion and the bear saw that the fox had stolen the deer, but as they couldn't follow they said: 'When two quarrel, the third profits.'

The literary and formal nature of the language of the Italian text of this fable suggests that the story was much, if not word for word, as she had learnt it at school. However, it did not seem appropriate to enquire how much of the original language was 'hers'; the important thing was that this was her contribution to the class, was read and discussed by the class and that this was clearly a source of great satisfaction to the student concerned.

I think it is important here to expand a little on what I mean by reading a story with the class. The aim is not an exercise in reading fluency, though this may be a 'side-effect', but to get to know intimately the shape, sentence-structure and narrative development of that particular text. I believe this is an important stage in developing the ability to construct a narrative oneself in another language. I am certainly not the first to state that reading is one of the most important ways of learning about writing.

Usually the reading would follow these stages:

1.   An initial presentation/discussion about who told the story, when, how and why, together with any other information the teller(s) may feel necessary. Unless the students are very used to doing this kind of work it may also be wise to point out that the story will be read in order to enjoy and discuss it, and not, for example, in order to do comprehension exercises on it. Again if necessary, it should be made clear that at least on the first reading they may not understand everything, and that they should not worry about this as plenty of time will be given to discussion and explanation.

2.   A copy of the text, preferably typed, is given to each student.

3.   The story (in English) is read in its entirety by the person who told it, or by myself if the student is not willing. The purpose of this is to get a feeling of the shape and structure of the story from the beginning (the method is probably only suitable for short texts like these). Students will follow the texts if they wish, or listen.

4.   Students will indicate which words and structures they find difficult. (I prefer not to teach vocabulary or potentially difficult grammar beforehand for the following reasons: so that students will not be distracted from the wholeness of the story by listening for particular words or phrases, and so that the students can select, discuss and interpret from context as a group what they wish to understand better.)

5.   The text will then be re-read and discussed for as long as the students wish. As they understand it better, other students will usually be willing to read aloud part of the text. Other versions of the story may be told at this stage, comparisons with other stories may be made, so it is as well to make sure there is plenty of time available.

6.   Students can then read the text again in pairs or groups.

7.   There should be an opportunity for reading the mother tongue text, if there is one, if the rest of the class wishes. Often students like to hear the sound of other languages, even if they don't understand them.

I believe this work made a great deal of difference to the atmosphere and relationships in this class; the students seemed more relaxed, interaction in English was more spontaneous and lively; this may have been how the dynamic of the class would have developed anyway, but I think this work helped. And the students all made good progress in their writing, and those who were able to write stories in

English did so: here is another story in the Nasreddin series that Figen wrote in English. The version given here is a corrected one which was written by Figen after I had worked through her original version with her, but it is very close to what she actually wrote the first time; Figen was different from the other students in the class in that what she wrote was usually more fluent and correct than what she said.

The cooking pot

There was an old man called Nasreddin. He was a very funny man. One day he asked his neighbour if he could borrow a big cooking pot.

After a day had gone by, Nasreddin gave his neighbour two cooking pots, one was slightly smaller than the other.

The neighbour asked: 'Why have you given me two cooking pots back?' Nasreddin replied to his neighbour: 'The large cooking pot you borrowed from me gave birth.'

The neighbour was very pleased. The next day Nasreddin went back to his neighbour and again asked if he could borrow his cooking pot. The neighbour gave it to him.

After days went by Nasreddin did not return his neighbour's cooking pot. He asked Nasreddin: 'Why have you not returned my pot to me?' Nasreddin replied: 'I am afraid your cooking pot has died.' The neighbour replied: 'How can a cooking pot die?'

Nasreddin replied: 'Well, you believed that your cooking pot gave birth, so why don't you believe that your cooking pot is dead?'

In conclusion, the following points should be considered:

1. The languages of the students were used in different ways and varying degrees in the stages of this work. On working through the Nasreddin tape later on with a Turkish speaker whose English is very fluent, it became clear that Shoray had never *told* the story in its entirety to Figen – they both knew it, after all. The Turkish parts of the tape consist of discussion about how the story should be told, discussion of detail and some prompting as to what came next. However the languages were used, it is doubtful whether any of this work could have taken place without them.

2. Students are usually very interested in each others' cultures and traditions. In this case the rest of the class were evidently quite happy to listen to quite long stretches of a language they did not understand (hardly a new experience for them, after all). It appeared that the activity was one which was considered important by the group. In more than one case the story was one which has versions in many languages. There was anticipation in the listening, the laughter was often prompted as much by recognition as surprise. It also seems to me that the texts produced are interesting and amusing in themselves, the kind of thing that anyone would enjoy reading and a way of solving the problem of finding good texts for the ESL class.

3. The use of the students' first languages is a constant reminder of their expressiveness and liveliness. Clearly much of the subtlety and complexity of the language is lost in telling in English. However, it seems that efforts to 'transfer' stories into English are appreciated, even if much is lost in the process.

4. Students will need to explain details which cannot be translated; for example, the Turkish-speaking students had to describe what a Hoca was and did. This is a genuine exercise in explaining and understanding explanations.

5. The development of creative writing and the valuing of students' languages and cultures as vital resources are processes (or parts of the same process) which depend on attitudes and relationships. The corollary of this is that initiatives of this kind will not always work. There will be times when no one wants to say or write anything, so one should be ready to accept this and to have other possibilities in mind. Equally, one should be ready to make room for stories when they turn up unexpectedly. Work of this kind depends on the interests and personalities of the people in the class and the relationships between these people: one can never predict how it will go. In this case, once the process of storytelling had started, many more stories were told, often in surprising ways.

Paulo Freire says: 'Intellectualist prejudices and above all class prejudices are responsible for the naive and unfounded notions that the people cannot write their own texts.' To this we could add, 'racist prejudices'. I believe that work of this nature is vital in the development of an anti-racist curriculum. Creativity – which involves the acknowledgment of the enormous resources of culture and language which students bring with them – is an essential element in establishing language learning which is truly adult.

References

Buckmaster, E. 'Developing basic reading and writing skills through the use of traditional stories', Materials pack for RSA/Dip/TESL/FACE 1982, unpublished.

ESL Publishing Group (ILEA), *ESL Issues 1: Mother Tongue and ESL*, London 1983.

Freire, P. *Cultural Action for Freedom*, Penguin 1972.

McLaughlin, J. 'Creative Writing in English as a Second Language Work' in *Viewpoints*, Issue No. 3, Adult Literacy and Basic Skills Unit, London 1985.

Another picture of an ESOL classroom is given in a case study of the perceptions of living and learning English in Blackburn, focusing on learners who are seeking asylum and refugee status (Hodge and Pitt, 2004). As part of this study Rachel Hodge was a participant observer in a number of sessions of an Entry 1 class, which she also audio-recorded. Analysis of her observation notes and the transcript showed diverse forms of peer learning support, encouraged by the teacher, Wendy. The use of the students' knowledge of various languages formed part of this support, and their own learning, as the following extract from the analysis shows:

> Part of this peer support for learning that is an integral feature of this classroom culture is the way Wendy allows the students freedom to use their linguistic resources which go beyond using their L1. The students often help each other's, and their own learning of English through the medium of their shared knowledge of other languages. The following description from Rachel's field notes of one particular activity using dictionaries illustrates this:

> > *Saeed asks Mohammed for some help – they speak in Farsi though Saeed's first language is Urdu.*
> > *Ferdinand writes Portuguese translation next to each word as he looks each one up in the English dictionary*
> > *Mohammed uses both Farsi and English dictionaries and both he and Faisullah write the Farsi word next to the English. Lisette writes English language definitions from the dictionaries next to each word*
> > *Saeed writes Urdu next to words*
> > *Joelle writes English language definitions from the dictionary*
> > *Omar writes Kurdish words and Kurdish definitions but is using an English dictionary*

Again, this practice is facilitated by the teacher. Wendy encourages Omar to sit with Ahmed who shares his own language (Kurdish). Although the classroom space is sometimes a multilingual one, the over-riding motivation these students have to learn English is ever-present:

> *Omar [the new student] and Ahmed are speaking to each other in their own language. Lisette [playfully] shakes her finger at Ahmed . . . and says 'you don't speak your own language in the class' . . . Ahmed: 'I explain him – it his first time in class.' The two Iraqi students continue to chat in their own language occasionally but this does not seem to interfere with their concentration*

They use their linguistic resources as one way to work towards this learning goal, and it is only one of their learning strategies. They also use English to help each other:

> *Lisette: I can't understand [looking at a picture of people socialising]*
> *Cristof: the girl, Nancy . . . girl's boring*

> *[Paula explaining 'far away' to Joelle] – Paula points to herself 'you near me', then points to Lisette. 'Lisette far away'*

(Hodge and Pitt, 2004, pp. 22–23)

These last two pieces of research depict some ESOL classrooms as places where speakers of diverse languages meet, and in some ways replicate the multilingual urban societies that are a feature of cities around the world, as discussed earlier in this chapter. In these classrooms, however, these rich linguistic resources may be used to enhance the learning of an additional language – English.

Discussion

1. What role is there for learners' first languages in the multicultural ESOL classroom, given that no space is allocated to them in the core curriculum?

2. What are your experiences of your own and your students' uses of code-switching? How does this linguistic behaviour relate to language learning?

3. Jane McLaughlin gives the following two reasons for encouraging the use of first languages in the learning of an additional one:

> For me the two main reasons have always been that the use of their own languages by the students means that they can use a wide range of learning strategies which are not available to them in the medium of English, and is therefore simply sound educational practice, and that the constant presence of other languages in the classroom prevents the culturally and linguistically intimidating effect of imposed monolingualism.
>
> (McLaughlin, 1986, p. 31)

Do you agree with her?

Can you think of other reasons for encouraging multilingual practices or arguments against such practices?

Research

Tape part of an ESOL class (with the students' permission) and transcribe the sections where students bring in their knowledge of other languages.

Can you identify the different ways that these resources are being used to support their learning?

An interesting way to do this would be to use the transcription as a basis for discussion with the students who were recorded.

Additional reading

Caldas, S. and Caron-Caldas, S. (2002) 'A sociolinguistic analysis of the language preferences of adolescent bilinguals: shifting allegiances and developing identities', *Applied Linguistics*, 23 (4): 490–514.

Crystal, D. (2004) *The Stories of English*, London: Allen Lane.

Chapter 4

Learning the written language
Cultures, communities and classrooms

Introduction

In this chapter we focus specifically on some of the issues involved in learning to read and write in an additional language. We start with debates about the degrees of similarity and difference between written languages and the practices they are embedded in. These discussions revolve around those learners who are already familiar with at least one writing system, and a set of literacy practices. How transferable are these practices from one language and writing system to another? We then move on to those learners who come from mainly oral cultures, or who have missed out on formal education and have very little experience of using the written systems of the languages they speak. Should these learners gain literacy in the languages they are really familiar with before taking on literacy in an additional language?

Issues surrounding the learning and teaching of the written language cover a wide area because writing systems are cultural constructs and vary considerably throughout the world. The readings in this chapter reflect this breadth. The extract from Richard Kern (Reading 1) gives us information about the range and nature of writing systems from the perspective of a linguist. This knowledge is useful for the language teacher who may be coping with mixed classes of learners who are used to a variety of different written languages. Jill Sinclair Bell's article (Reading 2) discusses in depth her own experience of learning a writing system that is culturally very distant from her first language. She writes from the positions of both learner and teacher. Reading 3, by Elsa Auerbach, comes out of community education, and sets out one particular methodology for the teaching of an additional written language.

Learning an additional literacy

Taking a social practice view of literacy

Many past studies of adults learning to read and write English have been based on autonomous notions of literacy, which Auerbach in the third reading defines as 'a set of isolated decoding skills to be acquired in an essentially similar universal process' (Auerbach, 1996, p. 9). Researchers asked questions about the transfer of reading and writing strategies from one written language to another, but they did not consider the cultural assumptions underlying particular uses of reading and writing. In many studies, literacy was seen as the mastering of a different script or writing system, alongside developing knowledge of syntax and vocabulary. There was little exploration of the ways in which the learners used their first written languages in different practices, and how these practices compared with those being taught in the new language.

Understandings of the ways reading and writing are culturally constructed and shaped by social practice are now helping to illuminate the processes of learning a new written language, as all three readings in this chapter show. In order for learners to understand the meaning of a text, they need to know more than how to decode the words and images that comprise it. Reading, for example, is a dynamic process of creating meaning from a set of symbols, and interpretation arises from a knowledge of the whole set of language use and choices of the social practice out of which the text is created.

Learning to read and write in another language involves learning *how* to interact with and construct particular kinds of texts, as well as increasing one's knowledge of vocabulary and structure. For example, university students from other countries participating in university courses in the UK or the USA find that the kinds of reading and writing they carried out successfully in their own countries may not be considered appropriate in their new sites of study. They not only have to grapple with expressing themselves in another language, they also find that the kinds of ideas they are expected to express, and the ways they are expected to read texts and write about them, may differ – a little or a lot – from their previous practices.

Learning another way of reading and writing is not, of course, restricted to learners of additional languages. We all find ourselves getting to grips with new conventions and expectations when we move into a new social world. However, those learners who go to live in another country and learn to use the majority written language have to cope with both learning the words and syntax of a new language and learning about the differing literacy practices they encounter.

The practice of critical reading

Catherine Wallace puts forward a critique of the kinds of reading and writing tasks often found in materials for English as a foreign language (EFL), and her critique is based on a social practice view of literacy (Wallace, 1992). In her account of her pedagogic practice with a mix of EFL and ESOL learners of English in London, she argues that texts are often separated from their social context and used as vehicles for linguistic structures. She encourages an awareness of different literacy practices by talking about the roles which reading played in the learners' lives, and getting them to interview family members about their reading. She also teaches the specific practice of critical reading of public literature such as newspapers, magazines and advertisements. (The word 'critical' here refers to social science work that is particularly interested in relationships between language and power; see e.g. Fairclough, 2003). Part of her approach is the posing of three questions before reading a text:

1. Why is this topic being written about?
2. How is the topic being written about?
3. What other ways of writing about the topic are there?

(Wallace, 1992, p. 71)

Wallace explores the language choices of public texts, such as the way the participants are named and the use of modality, in order to make apparent the discourses out of which the text is created (see Jessop *et al.* (1998) for more about this practice). She argues that the attention to grammatical structure which forms an integral part of formal language teaching may be drawn on to develop this critical reading practice. Reading, here, is more than decoding words; it focuses on exploring how media texts try to create particular meanings out of events.

Learning a new writing system

Although Wallace's classes contained a mix of Japanese and European learners, she does not discuss any cultural differences in the take-up of a new reading practice. Jill Sinclair Bell, on the other hand, focuses on the processes of becoming literate in a language where the writing system or script, and the cultural practices, differ considerably from the learner's first language(s) and culture. Through her experiences of learning how to write with the Chinese writing system, she argues that assumptions about learning and literacy acquired in one culture can actually act as a barrier to progress in learning the additional written language.

📖 Activity: Guided Reading

Reading 1:

Kern, R. (2000) 'Linguistic resources: writing systems and media', in *Literacy and Language Teaching*. Oxford: Oxford University Press, pp. 68–74.

Before exploring Bell's experiences and argument about learning a different writing system it might be a good idea to read Kern's discussion of different writing systems. He also discusses the visual features of written texts and the way they contribute to the meanings we make through the written language.

How do the visual features of written languages compensate for the incomplete nature of written communication?

Linguistic resources

The most fundamental of Available Designs is language itself. The most obvious and essential difference between reading and writing in one's native language versus a foreign language is that one is operating with a new set of linguistic resources. The writing system, phonological system, lexicon, syntax, semantic relations, and pragmatic conventions of the new language may differ considerably from those of the native language, and, even in the case of closely related languages, it takes years of study for learners to develop anything near the same level of linguistic comfort that they enjoy when using their native language. In this section we will briefly and selectively discuss linguistic resources, and consider some of the ways in which learners' existing linguistic Available Designs can promote (or hinder) the development of literacy and communicative ability in a new language.

Writing systems and media

The first thing that strikes beginning language students is the way the new language sounds and the way it looks on paper. In academic language study, the writing system is often an immediate point of focus, as it serves as the entry point for vocabulary and grammar study.

Coulmas (1989) makes a useful distinction between writing systems, scripts, and orthographies. Writing systems are not language-specific but are differentiated by the particular ways they segment and represent language (for example, ideographic versus alphabetic writing). Scripts are particular manifestations of a given writing system (for example, Roman, Greek, Arabic, Cyrillic alphabets) and may or may not be language-specific. Orthographies are language-specific conventions (for example, accents and other marks, spelling rules) that may differentiate among varieties within the language (for example, American versus British English, Chinese versus Taiwanese, or Standard German versus Swiss-German orthographies).

From a language learning perspective, some writing systems are simpler to process and learn than others. Alphabetic and syllabary systems, for example, have small symbol inventories. Even when one must learn an entirely new script (for example, an English speaker learning Cyrillic, Greek, Persian, Arabic, or Hebrew alphabets, the task is infinitely easier than learning an ideographic system that has thousands of distinct characters. Layout and directional processing conventions can also influence the difficulty of learning. Hebrew and Arabic, for example, are written and read from right to left. Chinese and Japanese are generally written and read in columns from top to bottom, proceeding from right to left. While reading and writing tend to be slower in a second language than in the first language because of increased attentional demands, the slowing effect is likely to be most pronounced in cases where one is learning a new writing system or script – and particularly troublesome in tasks that emphasize speed, such as skimming, scanning, dictation, and note-taking.

Another potentially problematic aspect of acquiring a new writing system or script is learning the parameters of variability in written forms. In all languages, written symbols often assume multiple forms depending on their position in a text or whether they are printed or handwritten. The printed letter 'a' for example, appears as 'A' at the beginning of a sentence or a name, and usually appears as something resembling 'a' in handwriting. In Arabic, some letters can assume up to four different shapes depending on their position in a word (Thompson-Panos and Thomas-Ruzic 1983). As shown in Figure 1, Chinese characters can be written in five styles of increasing degrees of cursivity: 'small seal', 'scribal', 'regular', 'running', and 'cursive'. To the uninitiated reader, the differences across these styles are much more striking than the resemblances, especially when one compares the endpoints of the stylistic continuum (i.e. 'small seal' and 'cursive').

Figure 1 The sentence 'Gold can be found in Lishui' written in five styles (from left to right): small seal, scribal, regular, running, and cursive (Coulmas 1989: 96)

As suggested in Chapter 1, familiarity with a language's writing system is essential for literacy, but that familiarity is useful only to the extent that one knows the *language* which the writing system represents. This is because any given writing system encodes only selected features of a language and leaves others unspecified. For example, Semitic alphabets, such as Arabic and Hebrew, consist only of consonants. While vowels are indicated by marks above or below the line of writing in pedagogical materials, these vowel markers are usually omitted, forcing the reader to rely extensively on the linguistic context to disambiguate word meanings (Pei 1965: 99). The Chinese writing system, on the other hand, makes no reference to the sound system at all and thus provides no clues for oral pronunciation. In sum, writing 'works' only when readers can compensate for what is *not* represented. As Coulmas puts it,

> The abstractness of writing is possible and functional because the typical reader – that is, the reader for whom the script is made – knows the language in which the written message is coded, and can thus rely on the redundancies of the language as an aid for deciphering (reading) written expressions which represent speech only incompletely or vaguely.
>
> (1989: 47)

Use of a writing system, then, requires familiarity not only with the script, but also with appropriate strategies that allow one to fill in unexpressed information, based on one's knowledge of the language.

The problem of compensating for what is not represented in a writing system extends beyond surface language structures. In his historical analysis of literacy, Olson (1994) concludes that, although different writing systems bring different dimensions of language into focus, they all succeed quite well in expressing what Austin (1962) called *locutionary acts* (i.e. what was said). However, one thing that no writing system does adequately, Olson argues, is specify the *illocutionary force* of such acts (i.e. how what was said was intended). Whereas speech generally provides multiple overt clues to the illocutionary force of an utterance (for example, through stress, intonation, tone of voice, as well as gestures, facial expressions, body language, and other features of the situational context), writing is much more limited in this capacity. Should we, for example, interpret 'Riders will mount their horses' as a prediction, as part of a future narrative, or as a command? Knowledge of the written code alone does not suffice – we must rely on a situational context, either real or imagined, in order to interpret this sentence. An essential problem of reading, then, is compensating for the absence of an immediate, shared context of communication which might clarify communicative intentions.

Olson's point meshes well with many teachers' observations that their students are generally quite good at identifying 'what the text says' but they often have a good deal of trouble understanding what it means – precisely because this is often not explicitly encoded in the text. While the point is well taken, it is nevertheless extremely important to bring to students' attention the various linguistic and graphic devices that writing *does* offer to express illocutionary force, however limited these may be. To convey emphasis in written English, for example, one can use typographical devices such as capitalization, italic and bold font styles, underlining, centering, or punctuation (for example, exclamation marks and asterisks). One can also use syntactic devices such as cleft constructions to simulate the effects of spoken stress (for example, 'It was a mushroom that Alice ate' compared with 'Alice ate a *mushroom*'). Verbs such as 'command', 'whisper', 'ask', 'bark', 'yell' and adverbs like 'sharply', 'soothingly', 'jokingly', and 'gravely' provide lexical means to suggest the tone of voice intended for stretches of written direct speech.

Punctuation, such as question marks and exclamation points, performs a similar function to intonation and stress in spoken language. Commas provide important clues about how the elements of a sentence are segmented. The phrase 'However you need to do it' means something very different from 'However, you need to do it'. The choice of dashes, commas, or parentheses can either accentuate or attenuate the importance of an embedded phrase:

> Linguistic communication – both oral and written – is multimodal in nature.
> Linguistic communication (both oral and written) is multimodal in nature.

And of course, we could further attenuate the embedded phrase by removing it from the sentence altogether and putting it in a footnote. It is important to recognize that punctuation conventions vary somewhat across languages. For example, Berman (1975: 249) points out that commas are normally required before 'that' clauses in Hebrew (for example, 'Some of them claimed, that the idea was impossible'), but that Hebrew does not observe the English convention of distinguishing restrictive and non-restrictive clauses by commas ('All the children, who do well in school, love to read' versus 'All the children who do well in school love to read'). Such differences in punctuation conventions are important to teach, since they can lead to confusion if learners are not aware of them.

. . .

Layout of print and typographical features can also provide important clues to meaning. Waller (1987) characterizes features such as headings, paragraphing, formatting, and typeface as 'macropunctuation at the discourse level' (p. 91), which directs readers' strategies and explains the organizational structure of a given text. Consider the difficulty you might have processing the following bit of text:

> It is the *interaction* of all these Available Designs, drawn upon by writers and readers operating in a given sociocultural context, that allows readers/writers to produce and interpret meaning through texts. Linguistic resources The most fundamental of Available Designs is language itself.

When it first appeared at the beginning of this section, however, it probably caused no difficulty at all because its particular formatting made the relationships among the elements clear (i.e. ending sentence, new section heading, first sentence of new section). Bernhardt (1991) showed that some of her American students of German had difficulty identifying who was writing to whom in a German letter because of errors in interpreting the formatting conventions of letters. Formatting conventions are clearly elements that teachers should bring to language students' attention, particularly in light of the fact that they sometimes differ across languages (Gremmo 1985; Régent 1985).

Finally, it is important to recognize that the physical location of texts can influence how they are interpreted. One might argue that a word is a word, wherever it might appear. But a moment's reflection leads one to realize that the physical situation of written words – whether on a computer screen, on a printed page, traced in a schoolchild's notebook, or displayed on a billboard – influences how we understand them and the reasons for their being written. The physical situation tells us something about how to read writing by providing clues about the relevant arena of language use (public versus private), the possible communicative intent (whether it is meant to inform us, persuade us, caution us, inspire us, touch us emotionally, and so on), and its relative permanence (for example, skywriting versus an inscription in stone). The physical situation can consequently influence our goals and actions: reading the word 'coffee' on a roadsign versus on a menu versus on a bag makes us do different things in response to our reading.

The point is that both speech and writing provide verbal and nonverbal clues to illocutionary force, but the clues are different – because speech and writing involve different media and are used in different social contexts. Language learners need to learn how speech and writing work differently to support the tacit relationship between speakers/listeners and readers/writers in acts of communication. They also need to learn what devices are appropriate for different contexts of written communication. Using 'smileys' in a formal letter or essay, for example, will not likely impress employers or teachers.

Learning to read and write thus involves a great deal more than mastery of the writing system – it involves a broader ability to understand relationships of visual and verbal forms in contexts of written communication. It involves creating 'discourse worlds' mediated by a variety of linguistic and nonlinguistic devices and conventions. Teachers play an important role in promoting students' understanding of these devices and conventions so they can use them appropriately to improve their ability to read and write in a second or foreign language.

Kern's reading explains some of the cultural variability inherent in different writing systems and scripts. Bell writes about her experiences of some of these differences in Reading 2. She describes how she set about learning to read and write the Chinese characters with the same beliefs and study techniques she used to learn and progress in Canadian education. She soon found, however, that her tutor had a different set of expectations and teaching methods. Neither Bell, nor her Chinese tutor Cindy Lam, realized the need to articulate their deep beliefs at the outset, and this resulted in much misunderstanding. Bell describes Cindy Lam, as holding 'two different stories of literacy in the two languages' (Bell, 1993, p. 470). Lam was bilingual in English and Chinese, having spent her first eleven years in Hong Kong, before moving to Canada. Hence her early schooling was in Cantonese, and her later schooling in English. She was an experienced teacher of English as an additional language but had not taught the Chinese written language before participating as the literacy tutor in Bell's research.

Bell records how Lam was surprised that she found herself teaching the Chinese characters as she herself had been taught. She found that both her own and Lam's beliefs about the way to learn to write were intimately bound up with the cultural beliefs about literacy, teaching and learning of their childhood.

📖 Activity: Guided Reading

Reading 2:

Bell, J. S. (1995) 'The relationship between L1 and L2 literacy: some complicating factors', *TESOL Quarterly*, 29 (4): 691–702.

You may want to read Bell's account now. As a result of this research Bell argues that it is essential for teachers to make their classroom procedures explicit and to raise awareness of different assumptions underlying understandings about literacy and learning.

What are some of your assumptions about literacy and learning? Are they the same as Bell's as she describes them in this article?

Background to the study

The initial pilot study for this project (see Bell, 1991) involved two adult Afghan males attempting initial English language literacy. Although generating some interesting insights, this pilot study clearly demonstrated the difficulty of asking academically unsophisticated subjects for rigorous self-analysis of learning patterns and assumptions, particularly when interrogated through an interpreter. Essentially, the information collected from this pilot study related only to behavioral patterns such as difficulties in copying material from a text or blackboard. What I wanted to discover was the ways in which people understood the task of literacy and the surprises they encountered when working with the literacy of a different language and different culture. The eventual study was consequently reframed into an auto-biographical L2 literacy attempt.

The basic theoretical framework for interpretation of this work was drawn from the literature of narrative research, (see, e.g., Carr, 1986; Clandinin & Connelly, 1986; Connelly & Clandinin, 1988; Crites, 1971; Hardy, 1975; Polkinghorne, 1988; White, 1973.) Such an approach acknowledges the life history of the research participants and fits particularly well with cross-cultural endeavors.

The work this article describes was originally carried out for a doctoral dissertation (Bell, 1991). I was consequently able to devote 12 months to the study of Chinese and the observation of that learning process. I arranged to study Chinese literacy with a private tutor, and simultaneously enrolled in a university course in spoken Cantonese, to build a lexical and syntactic base from which the study of Chinese characters could draw.

I was fortunate to find Cindy Lam, a highly experienced ESL colleague for my literacy tutor. Cindy is bilingual and bicultural, having been born in Hong Kong and having had all her early education there, in Cantonese. She came to Canada as an adolescent and completed high school, university, and teacher education here. Despite her considerable ESL teaching experience, Cindy had never before taught Chinese literacy, although she had taught English literacy to a number of Chinese students.

The study

My study of Chinese involved two rather different literacy experiences. In the spoken Cantonese course, I was a member of a class which originally included 28 people and which dwindled over the course of the academic year to an enrollment of five (four ethnic Chinese and myself.) My studies in this oral language course took shape in ways which were largely familiar and expected. We were introduced to new material in recorded dialogues followed by exercises to practice the new vocabulary and grammar patterns. The teacher presented the language as an organized system, stressing the relationships between common items and pointing out the underlying structures. In these classes I discovered that my working patterns were much like those documented in a number of autobiographical accounts of L2 learning (see, e.g., Bailey & Ochsner, 1983; Savignon, 1983; Schumann & Schumann, 1977). I found myself unduly concerned with my public performance in class and prone to measure my progress comparatively against that of my peers. In what appears to be a fairly common pattern, I passed through the stages of initial confidence and interest, followed by sudden concern as the language became more difficult, settling finally into a level of comfort as the class developed a sense of group identity.

In this spoken Cantonese course, we worked from a textbook which used Yale Romanization to transcribe Cantonese pronunciation of Chinese characters. For example, the characters meaning I am Chinese would be transcribed in Yale as Ngóh haih Jùnggwok yàhn. This method of transcription allowed me and the other class members to work with written versions of recorded dialogues, manipulate sentence patterns, and complete written exercises. Although I had difficulty in producing the appropriate word tone as indicated by the diacritics, in almost all other ways, I found my English language literacy to be of tremendous help in working with this literacy-based task. Being able to read the written form of a dialogue helped me clarify what

I was hearing on a tape. Seeing similarities of written form helped me recognize the relationships between similar sounding words. Above all, having a way to record for my own reference the new words I was learning allowed me to bring all my study skills to bear on the new task I was attempting. There was no doubt that my L1 literacy skills were proving useful in this environment.

However, the situation was rather more complicated in the other literacy experience, that is in the tutorials in which I was learning Chinese characters. Here my L1 literacy skills often seemed to be a stumbling block rather than an advantage. I approached the task of Chinese literacy with the unconscious assumption that I could learn it in the same way I had learned to read and write in English. I assumed that a learning style which had given me success in an English language school system would be appropriate here. I assumed that I would recognize progress when I made it. I assumed I knew what literacy was for and how it was demonstrated. Over the course of the next 12 months I eventually discovered that I was mistaken in all these assumptions.

The differences between Cindy's and my understandings of literacy were not immediately apparent. In our initial planning, we both drew on our experiences as ESL literacy teachers, as we discussed the relative merits of methodologies such as Total Physical Response and Language Experience Approach. For our first lesson, Cindy planned a variety of activities to maintain my interest, including some Cantonese popular songs for me to listen to. She made every effort to create a learner-centered lesson asking me what I wanted as a learner, particularly providing me with the option of such individualized activities as working with my name.

However, once Cindy began to teach me Chinese characters, she began to think in Chinese about literacy, and largely to her own surprise, she found herself teaching in accordance with her understanding of Chinese literacy, rather than in the way she usually teaches English literacy. Not surprisingly, Cindy's understanding of Chinese literacy reflected the way she had learned to read and write as a child.

Describing her early school days, Cindy commented that she remembered very little explicit instruction from the teacher. She learned to read and write essentially by copying from a primer – first individual characters and later model sentences. The characters were presented in order of their complexity, with the simple strokes of the numerals providing the first introduction. She taught me by essentially the same method. A typical introduction would be for her to present a model character, demonstrate the stroke order for me, then ask me to reproduce it myself. For homework, I would practice the characters many times over, using squared paper designed for children.

It seemed to me at the time that we made very slow progress during the first 3 or 4 months. She would introduce me to perhaps four new characters in a week, sometimes less. I would practice these characters over and over, to the point where I felt that I knew them thoroughly, yet never apparently to Cindy's satisfaction.

Her feedback generally consisted of asking me to practice them some more. She commented on the lack of balance in the characters, and on the need for total concentration when writing them. She urged me to work only in ideal conditions which included a quiet room and a clean desk so that concentration was possible. Struggling as I was under the time pressures of transcribing tutorials and oral classes, annotating transcripts, and completing journals, I was uneasily aware that very little of my homework was done under such conditions.

Around this time, I became concerned about the lack of progress I was apparently making. I did not understand what Cindy meant when she said that my characters needed balance and pressed her to give me more specific feedback about the shape the characters should take. I found it difficult to work from handwritten models which all varied in subtle ways and made it hard to identify which features were key to the character and which were individual stylistic flourishes. I plagued Cindy with questions about the exact relationship between strokes, asking for instance whether Stroke 2 should intersect Stroke 1 exactly at the midpoint or lower down. Her response to such questions was normally that the difference was not significant and that I should simply practice the characters more and the balance would come.

In my oral classes, by this time I had reached the point where I could understand or produce a short conversational passage transcribed in the Yale Romanization. I was eager for Cindy to teach me the appropriate characters to accompany this oral competence so that I could move on to writing more challenging pieces. I tallied up my meager word count – some 20 characters after 2 months of study – and wondered why we were proceeding so slowly. I began to feel like a failure and to resent feedback which was largely framed in phrases such as "losing your concentration" or "lacking balance."

It is hard to describe how stressful this early part of the study was for me. I had gone into the study with certain expectations of myself as a learner based on fairly successful school experiences. I believed I knew how to study and what kind of work teachers would require of me. I was confident that with effort I could achieve success in this academic endeavor. And yet, here I was, devoting all my waking hours, (and considerable amounts of my dream time) to the task and yet failing to achieve any measure of success that I could recognize. The result was a major shock to my image of self, which manifested itself in various bodily ways consistent with severe stress. The more distressed I became, the more I intensified my efforts to succeed and the more I fell back on the ways of learning which had served me well in previous learning experiences.

Differences in understanding of the literacy process

Ultimately, I came to realize that this pattern of previous learning success was the very thing which was holding me back from progress. I had assumed that I could approach Chinese literacy in the way in which I had learned and taught English language literacy. Instead I had to realize that Chinese literacy was a very different matter from English language literacy, requiring a different learning style. I recognize that what I describe below is drawn from the very personal experiences of two people, and as such I cannot assume that all cross-cultural learners will share this experience. However, I believe that a significant portion of what I describe is drawn from Cindy's and my cultural backgrounds rather than our personal ones. As such, these areas of difficulty suggest a culture-specific view of literacy which should illuminate our understanding of the task which L2 learners from widely different cultures face.

Literacy as reading versus literacy as writing

One assumption which gave me immediate difficulty was the ultimate goal of my literacy efforts. Over time it became evident that I had unconsciously assumed I would learn Chinese characters primarily in order to read Chinese text. I wanted to be able to write also, but in the time available for the study I was unlikely to achieve sufficient fluency to be writing for a Chinese audience. Given this primary focus on reading, I considered a word learned when I could recognize, understand, and pronounce the character, and when I could produce it on paper generating the correct strokes in the correct order. I found it rather baffling then, when after demonstrating the ability to produce characters in this way, Cindy would ask me to continue practicing the same characters. Instead I wanted to move on to new characters so that I could increase my vocabulary. Similarly, I wanted to choose the characters I learned according to their meaning, selecting those most likely to appear in menus, street signs or other environmental print.

For Cindy, however, literacy definitely meant writing. Describing her initial experiences with literacy she said:

> 1. *Cindy*: I had so much of it as a kid . . . a lot of it was writing. You really didn't get into much reading, first you had to learn every single character you read.
> *Jill*: Learn in the sense of writing?
> *Cindy*: Writing yes, and remembering it. I associate literacy in Chinese so much with writing and less with reading.

Working from this understanding of literacy, Cindy selected characters for me to learn based on the difficulty of their strokes rather than on their meaning. She did not consider characters learned simply because I could read them and produce an approximation of them on paper. Consequently, she expected me to continue to work on the same characters until I was able to write them to her satisfaction.

This would not have been problematic had either of us made our expectations clear to the other. Unfortunately our assumptions about the purpose of what we were doing were still largely unconscious and as such not open to formal scrutiny.

Form and content

Another major difference in our views of literacy concerned the significance we attached to the form of a written message and the relationship of that form to the content. When Cindy began to teach me with a methodology which worked largely toward improving my writing of the characters, I was baffled and frustrated. For Cindy, learning the correct strokes of a character was merely the beginning of the process. The next step was to practice the known character over and over again to help to develop the appearance of one's writing.

I found this insistence on form somewhat frustrating. Early on in the study, Cindy gave me a short dictation test. At first, I was rather pleased with my performance as I knew all the words she dictated and quickly wrote down the appropriate characters somewhat smugly. When Cindy looked at the result, she did not praise my demonstrated ability to generate the correct characters. Instead she gently pointed out that in my haste I had let the quality of my characters slip. My journal records that "I felt as if I had been marked wrong in a multiple choice test because my check mark went out of the box."

Initially, I understood Cindy's focus on form as merely comparable to English handwriting practice. I assumed that I would write more attractively as I became more practiced with the characters and did not understand why this practice could not take place with a rich range of characters rather than with a small restricted vocabulary. Cindy tried to explain the importance of form to me, saying:

> 2. Calligraphy or penmanship – isn't important in English. It's not the writing, it's the knowing and the recognizing that's important. But in Chinese, it's the writing art that is as much a part of literacy as the reading.

It eventually became apparent that for Cindy, form was a key vehicle for presentation of the self. The appearance of one's writing made evident to the reader the kind of personality one had and the degree to which balance and discipline were developed. She talked about one's characters being "part of oneself," and how they "show one to the world." This thinking was in direct contrast to my assumption that the content of what I wrote was the vehicle by which I displayed myself to others, while form was relatively unimportant. My attitude is certainly not unusual in North American society, as is indicated by our tolerance for poor handwriting on the part of physicians, who lose little prestige even when their writing is unintelligible. After the study was over, Cindy commented,

3. I thought even if you were doing it for your thesis, I felt you should go through the same thing I went through, you ought to be proud of your characters. Maybe there was something that I had – something within me but never articulated – something never even actually told to me. But I think I did know deep down what the definition of literacy was in Chinese, and it had a lot to do with how you produced the characters.

As well as having different understandings of the value of form, we also saw a different relationship between form and content. My approach to learning Chinese literacy indicated I perceived a split between form and content. On those occasions where improvement of form was necessary, I believed it could be attended to after the content was decided. This pattern was made evident by ways of working such as drafting out the content of a journal piece while riding the subway and then producing a fair copy of the characters later. Again, this is a pattern widely encouraged in the North American school system where we encourage children to produce rough drafts and then edit their work.

For Cindy, form and content were inseparable. For her, "the form of a text is inextricably linked to the content." Cindy explained that her teachers felt it was not acceptable to develop the ideas and then try to work on the form. She commented, "When I was in school, my teachers always insisted that the flow of ideas and the development of form should be concurrent. It's too late by the time you have got the ideas out to go back and look at the form." She acknowledged that "ideas are important" but continued "ideas have to be shaped in such a way – it's the presentation, not *just* the idea." As a result, she was distressed that I would scribble out first drafts of my pieces and then later try to copy them out. By working in this way, I gave myself no opportunity to develop the kind of mental discipline and balance that she believed was a key part of literacy.

Characteristics of a good learner

The third major area in which I found that my LI literacy patterns were interfering with my progress was that of learning style. Obviously this is an area where, individual personality plays a part, but the major patterns I demonstrated are those which are favorably regarded in most Canadian schools and as such may be considered typical of many learners from our culture. I worked as quickly as the demands of accuracy allowed. I tried to be an active learner, demonstrating commitment and engagement. Above all, I approached the task as one which was inherently systematic, searching for indications of rules and patterns which could be applied in other contexts. Most of these features of my learning style were to prove an impediment to good progress in Chinese literacy.

Speed was the first issue which came under challenge. In my memories of learning as a child, it seemed that speed was always praised or rewarded – children who finished assignments quickly were complimented and given free choice of activities, for example. However, Cindy did not see speed as being relevant or helpful to the development of literacy in Chinese. In our very first lesson, she made this clear. As she watched me writing characters she commented, "You're doing the strokes so quickly. . . . You're rushing through them. It doesn't matter how many you do. You just have to do them well. . . . So do them slowly." Throughout the study she would make comments such as "I'd rather you did three sentences well, than seven sentences badly." She was similarly unimpressed when I wrote long journal pieces or read text aloud rapidly. Despite this explicit feedback, I found it difficult to let go of the idea that speed could be a valuable asset in the classroom. Obviously I heard what Cindy was saying to me, but somehow I could not quite accept it. I slowed down when attempting very specific tasks, especially while she was watching me, but essentially for the first part of the study, I continued without any significant change.

My assumption regarding the value of being an active, questioning learner was also challenged. The transcripts show that I was constantly commenting on the process, questioning Cindy about the applicability of an example to other contexts, commenting on similarities I saw and so on. The transcripts of our lessons are probably one of the few examples of student–teacher interaction where the learner talks more than the teacher. Some of this is no doubt merely personal garrulity, but again, student engagement as demonstrated in active questioning is a pattern largely encouraged and rewarded in our school system. However, Cindy's traditional story of education was that "the way to learn is to receive," which she elaborated to "You do a lot of observing and then you think about it." Cindy never tried to silence me or put me down for this chattiness; but neither did she find it a particularly helpful way for us to proceed. She had not been taught Chinese literacy in an environment where the teacher was constantly questioned. Consequently she found it difficult to respond to many of my comments. "You are asking questions the answers to which I have never thought about," she said on one occasion.

Analytic versus holistic approaches

Closely related to Cindy's difficulties in answering this barrage of questions was the difference between the analytic learning style I was making use of and her holistic understanding of Chinese literacy. Much of my rushing into verbalization was an attempt to think out the relationships between new information and prior knowledge, or an attempt to break down an incomprehensible unit into pieces which I could classify and manipulate.

I am somewhat baffled by my deep-rooted assumption that analysis was the route to follow, as I work more holistically in nonacademic endeavors, such as painting or learning new music. The most likely explanation seems to be that my Western education has trained me to work in a certain way when approaching academic tasks. Certainly I was taught my L1 literacy through a pattern of analysis where words were broken down into letters and letters into lines and curves. Similarly, the ability to break word sounds down into phonemes was key to the way I learned to write in English.

This pattern was very evident in my attempts to learn the pronunciation of the characters. Just as Cindy modeled characters as whole units, so she tried to teach me the sound of the characters by modeling the word for me to imitate. The transcripts show that my immediate reaction was not to repeat the word but to push Cindy to be more specific about it.

> 4. *Cindy*: *Chut, chut*
> *Jill*: There's something I can hear there apart from the *t* and the vowel. What is it? *Tsc? ts? ch?* Is it like aspirated *t*?
> *Cindy*: No, it's like *hut, –chut, chut*
> *Jill*: Is there a consonant at the end?

However, Cindy had not been taught these characters and their sounds by analysis but by constant repetition of the whole unit. Many of the sounds had no direct English equivalent. What I was asking her to do was comparable to demanding the correct spelling of the sound made by a hiccup. This particular conversation continues for many pages in the transcript. Throughout, I ask similarly analytic questions, while avoiding doing what Cindy actually asked of me, which was to repeat the word.

This search for a system underlying the language was by no means restricted to the pronunciation. I have mentioned how I asked for tight specifications on character production. I was similarly sure there had to be a system underlying the syntax rules and was constantly overgeneralizing scraps of knowledge. If the knowledge could be reduced to a rule-based system, I felt confident of my ability to get control of it. I took pride in my ability to analyze and synthesize, look for patterns, and find connections between apparently discrete pieces of knowledge.

The following discussion of the importance of correct stroke order captures nicely our different approaches.

> 5. *Cindy*: I couldn't produce a good character if I made the right hand stroke before the left.
> *Jill*: Your hand would be traveling the wrong way.
> *Cindy*: Well, I wouldn't be able to create the same feeling of unity in the word.

Measures of progress and ideas of feedback

It took some months before remarks like the one above had much meaning for me. I could not really understand what Cindy was asking of me when she urged me to try for balance and unity, so I was not capable of measuring my progress in these areas. Instead, I assigned myself goals based on the kind of progress I had seen my ESL students demonstrate. I thought about characters as if they were English sight words to be learned in their entirety as a pattern. I assumed that each new character would take the same amount of time to learn as the early ones did. Thus if I learned only 4 characters in the first week, I expected to learn 40 characters in 10 weeks and so on. Somehow, I did not see that I was developing a considerable amount of implicit knowledge that could not be represented in this simple character or word counting measure of progress. I was learning the underlying parameters of the system, the basic strokes from which many characters are made, some elementary syntax, and so on. Obviously in the early stages of the learning, one is being heavily challenged by all these demands, and yet I was taken by surprise and failed to recognize what was happening. Presumably, those learning English for the first time have to make similar progress in terms of learning letter shapes, print conventions, and basic syntax so that their progress would also be slow initially. However, I did not allow for this in my own study. I can only assume that my basic belief was that all my English language and literacy knowledge could be transferred, so that I saw the entire learning task as conquering these particular visual shapes.

My assumptions as to what constituted acceptable progress were so powerful that they shaped the way I heard and interpreted Cindy's feedback. As I have transcripts of all our tutorials, I can look back and see a number of occasions where she commented favorably on my progress in those first weeks. However, I completely discounted her remarks and was seriously distressed about my limited progress.

It also became apparent that we had different stories for understanding teacher remarks. As an ESL teacher I tend to give out praise for effort as a means of encouragement. Cindy gives out praise as an acknowledgment of achievement. Consequently, what she saw as explicit, obvious praise, I saw as a meaningless routine courtesy. I took it for granted, therefore, that she was as dissatisfied with my progress as I was.

I was unhappy and discouraged at this point. I was failing by my own standards, and I did not understand what Cindy was trying to teach me. The more confused I got, the more I fell back on those patterns of learning which had proved successful for me in the past. It did not occur to me that part of the problem was the way I was approaching the task and that maybe Chinese literacy required a different approach. Instead I relied on the strategies which had brought me success with English language literacy, intensifying my efforts but achieving less and less.

But as I eventually and somewhat painfully came to realize, this is not the only way to approach literacy. By focusing my attention on the figure rather than the ground, or the part rather than the whole, I was learning a different kind of literacy. Before I could make the kind of progress which Cindy wanted for me, I had to change my assumptions about what learning and literacy consisted of. I was to find that this was a stressful experience.

Conclusions

As a learner I was in a highly privileged position compared with the vast majority of literacy students in North America. I did not need to become literate in Chinese in order to find work or support my family. I had confidence in my ability to learn, a settled home life, and helpful teachers who spoke my language. Despite all these advantages, I found this experience immensely stressful and can only imagine the effect on those with less support.

Most of my difficulties arose out of my mistaken assumption that literacy in English and Chinese was differentiated only by the shape of the squiggles on the paper. Consequently I used the same strategies and approaches for L2 literacy as had given me success in L1 literacy. The resultant failures left me baffled and frustrated. Had I realized I was attempting to develop a new way of thinking, learning a new way to present myself to the world, and developing a new set of values, I might have been more prepared for the impact this would have on my sense of identity.

What was this new way of thinking, these new values? The process of coming to understand even the beginnings of what Cindy meant when she spoke of qualities such as balance and concentration is not one which I can neatly sum up in a few sentences. Part of my difficulty in working in the ways which Cindy valued, and certainly in trying to write about the experience, was that I had no language to express the concepts she was trying to teach me, so that any vocabulary I used seemed either loaded or inadequate. At one point I attempted to explain the challenge by suggesting that I was trying to move from being a left brain learner to a greater reliance on the use of the right brain. This may be neurologically true but it only skims the surface of what I am trying to express.

The simplest honest statement I can make is that I eventually came to understand concentration as something more akin to the mental state one reaches through meditation than to the active, questioning, analytic mental mode which I had previously understood the word to mean. This shift required a considerable change in the way I approached literacy, and in the qualities of self I felt my literacy would portray. (See Bell, 1991, for more discussion of this issue.)

It is no doubt possible to learn to read and write in Chinese by methods which essentially allow one to transcribe English thinking via Chinese characters. Such an ability should not be confused, however, with developing Chinese literacy. In the same way, ESL literacy teachers have to recognize that they are teaching far more than the letters of the alphabet. I have suggested above that we need to think about the relationship between form and content and that between part and whole. We need to become conscious of our notions of how progress is measured and how it is rewarded. We need to consider the human qualities which are valued in our society and explore how these are made manifest in our preferred literacy practices. We need to explore our own assumptions and recognize that much of what we used to consider an inherent part of literacy is actually culturally imposed. Until we become aware of the unspoken assumptions we hold about literacy in English, we will be unable to introduce our students to full English language literacy.

Bell gives us a vivid personal account of additional literacy learning and the deep relationships between culture and the written language. Of course, the materiality and processes of writing are now being changed by new technology and the widespread use of the keyboard, but we can find cultural variability even in this supposedly uniform system of printed characters and fonts. Kern, for example, compares the forms and uses of 'emoticons' across cultures. Emoticons are used to represent facial expressions in e-mails and internet chat rooms, and Kern shows how Japanese emoticons differ from those in the USA and Europe:

Table 4.1 Differences between Japanese and Western emoticons (Based on Pollack, 1996)

Japan		USA and Europe	
Smiles			
Regular smile	(^-^)	regular smile	:-)
Very happy	(^0^)	very happy	:-))
Banzai smiley	\(^-^)/	wink	;-)
Girl's smile	(^.^)		
Other emotions or states			
Cold sweat	(^^;)	angry	:-ll
Excuse me	(^0^>)	sad	:-(
Exciting	(*^0^*)	wow!	:-o

The Japanese 'smiley' is more immediately recognizable as a face than the Western version because it is right side up rather than rotated to the left. But because the 'mouth' line does not curve up at the ends, it is less obviously a 'smile'. Particularly interesting is the 'girl's smile', in which the mouth is represented by a dot, reflecting the politeness norm of women not baring their teeth in a grin. The 'banzai' smiley represents arms raised in an ebullient cheer. 'Cold sweat' and 'excuse me' (the most popular Japanese emoticons) use the semicolon for dripping sweat and the > symbol to represent the bent arm of an embarrassed or apologetic person scratching the back of his or her head. According to Pollack (1996), the Japanese use emoticons more frequently than Westerners do in their electronic communications, perhaps because of their habitual use of pictograms, or perhaps because of their particular reliance on facial expressions and contextual features to express what is not explicitly expressed verbally. As one official at a Japanese online information service put it, 'If it's only words, it's hard to express your feeling to the other party' (Pollack 1996: C5). Pollack points out, however, that the Japanese tend not to use emoticons that express *emotions* such as surprise, anger or sadness, as they might potentially offend one's correspondent.

(Kern, 2000, p. 72)

We can see from this comparison that cultural norms can even shape the standardized forms of written language which come with the new information technologies.

Learners with little experience of the written language

Not all adult language learners arrive in the classroom with experience of one or more written languages. Some groups of learners have not had the opportunity of a consistent formal education, while others come from predominantly oral cultures. The pedagogic debate about such learners is whether to go straight into teaching both oral and written English, or to introduce learners to the written mode of the language they are already familiar with first, and then transfer to reading and writing in English.

In practice, non-literate learners are often placed in the same classes as those with modest or high levels of experience with a written language. For example, a large American project, 'What Works', tracking the progress of 495 adult ESOL learners with less than six years of formal education and low scores on literacy tests, found that, in the first cohort, the majority were in mixed literacy-level classes (American Institutes for Research, 2001). Similarly, as part of her research into literacy learning, Bell was a participant observer of a full-time twelve-week, pre-basic ESOL class in a Canadian government centre for recently arrived immigrants. The learners had very mixed levels of literacy, and included two migrants from Afghanistan with no experience of the written mode (Bell, 1997). In both of these research projects, the literacy instruction observed was limited. In the Canadian class learners mainly copied words and learned to recite short dialogues. In the American classrooms instruction was largely copying from the board and the teaching of phonics.

In the UK Melanie Cooke investigated an EFL and an ESOL course in one London college (Cooke, 2000). She argued that neither course met the literacy needs of the learners. The EFL course was based on the assumption that the learners had experience of post-school literacy practices, which was not always the case. The learners on the ESOL course had mixed levels of experience with the written modes. The ESOL teachers did not have training to help those with little experience, but at the same time the course was too basic for those learners with a lot of experience in using the written mode of their home languages.

Biliteracy approaches

Where there are larger communities of learners sharing the same languages and cultures, bilingual programmes have been set up, as already discussed in Chapter 3. In the USA some of these programmes offer learners instruction in the written mode of their home language alongside classes in spoken English. For example, a community project was set up in the Boston area in 1989. This was based on collaboration between the University of Massachusetts and three different community centres; one serving a large Central American population and refugees from Cambodia, another serving Haitian immigrants and refugees, and a third serving over twenty-six nationality and language groups. Reading 3 in this chapter, by Elsa Auerbach, explains the theoretical approach and methodologies of this project.

A key element of this programme in two of the community centres was an introduction to literacy through the learners' home languages. One of the rationales for this approach is that the oral language knowledge of the learners is a vital basis for learning literacy. This viewpoint is supported by Richard Kern's description of the limitations of all writing systems in Reading 1. As he points out, the written mode of any language cannot be an exact representation of the spoken mode. All systems are selective in their encoding of the oral language, and it is our familiarity with that language and the culture it is embedded in which helps us fill the gaps when we read, or construct appropriate text as we write.

This integral relationship between orality and literacy is supported by the findings of the American 'What Works' research project, mentioned above. This project tested the informants' spoken and written English at the beginning of their entry into an ESOL programme, and three and nine months later. They found that learners with higher initial levels of oral English made more progress in reading (no learner in this study made significant progress in writing).

Coming to grips with the essentially abstract nature of the written language, and how writing transforms meaning, is less daunting when adult learners can draw on their familiarity with the spoken language and culture. Auerbach, in Reading 3, also argues that offering bilingual and biliterate instruction reduces the anxiety of learners who have had little experience of formal education, and attracts those learners who have previously dropped out of ESOL provision. However, elsewhere in her evaluation of these programmes, she lists the practical challenges that such a programme encounters. For example, there is a problem with the lack of classroom materials for literacy instruction in languages other than English. A biliteracy approach also creates the need for more teachers and classes, since there need to be transitional classes where learners move towards English literacy.

Activity: Guided Reading

Reading 3:

Auerbach, E. (1996) *From the Community to the Community: A Guidebook for Participatory Literacy Training*, Mahwah, NJ: Lawrence Erlbaum, pp. 9–12, 16–18.

You may want to read Auerbach's explanation of the participatory approach to biliteracy programmes now.

How do the students' lives drive the curriculum in this approach?

How is this model supported by theory and research?

Although the rationale for our model arose directly from the concrete conditions, needs, and initiatives at the sites, we were by no means alone in arriving at these conclusions. There is substantial justification for each of the key features of the model from a wide range of other sources. This support comes from language acquisition and literacy theory and research, as well as from the work of other practitioners and projects both nationally and internationally. The next sections briefly examine some of the research, theory, and practice, indicating why each of these project's key features is educationally sound.

Why a meaning-based, culturally variable view of literacy?

Cultural variability in literacy practices

The past decade has seen advances in the theoretical understanding of the nature of literacy, and, in particular, of the ways it varies according to culture and context. Studies of literacy practices in a range of cultures indicate variation in types of texts, participant interactions around texts, purposes for creating and using texts, social meanings/values attached to texts, ways of producing texts, and ways of socializing children through interactions with texts. A new paradigm has emerged in which literacy is viewed not just as a set of isolated decoding skills to be acquired in an essentially similar universal process, but rather as a set of social practices that vary according to cultures, contexts, purposes, and participants. This means that culture-specific aspects of language and literacy use must be taken into account in literacy programming and curriculum development; wherever possible, teachers must be aware of culture-specific discourse practices, literacy uses and forms of learners' cultures (Heath, 1983; Reder, 1987; Street, 1984; Taylor and Dorsey-Gaines, 1988).

Connections between oral and written language

Another aspect of this emerging paradigm is that, increasingly, the divide between oral and written language has come to be questioned. Older views claimed that literacy was unique in that it allowed meaning to be represented autonomously, without reference to context; recent studies show that, in fact, there are many features of what has traditionally been thought of as oral discourse in written language and vice versa. A new conception of *literacies* has emerged in which a variety of discourse forms are seen to encompass a range of features of both oral and written language. Culture-specific uses of oral language shape the way that learners take and make meaning through texts. Teachers must draw on learners' oral language practices in developing their reading and writing (Gee, 1990; Tannen, 1982; Street, 1984).

Literacy acquisition as a meaning-making process

Further, this paradigm claims that literacy acquisition involves not just mechanically connecting sounds and symbols, but making meaning by interacting with texts. Reading and learning to read are active, constructive processes, as are writing and learning to write: learners bring their own knowledge to texts in order to make sense of them. Culture plays a role in learning: learners' cultural familiarity with the content and forms of texts shape their reading processes. Learners become proficient to the extent that instruction is connected to their background knowledge, life experiences, and communicative purposes. Traditional approaches that focus on the individual's acquisition of skills without consideration of social context disconnect literacy acquisition from learners' knowledge and lived experience. Thus, it is critical that instruction be meaning-centered, rather than mechanical, and that content be relevant to the life experiences of learners (Carrell and Eisterhold, 1983; Street, 1984).

Connections between the word and the world

Current literacy theory suggests that literacy is meaningful for learners to the extent that it enables them to better understand and shape their world. Brazilian educator

Paulo Freire says that there must be a connection between the **word** and the **world** (Freire and Macedo, 1987). Mechanical approaches that focus on the acquisition of isolated skills without consideration of the social conditions of learners' lives disconnect literacy acquisition from their knowledge, concerns, and experiences. As literacy educator Susan Lytle (1991) says, "Being and becoming literate means using knowledge and experience to make sense of and act on the world" (p. 8). In the approach proposed by Freire (1970), instruction starts with learners' social reality, providing a context for analyzing it and taking action on it. If literacy acquisition is linked with this kind of critical analysis, it can enable learners to challenge the social conditions that disempower them. Thus, literacy instruction should involve exploration of the social issues and concerns of learners' lives.

So what?

Findings from this theoretical and practical work suggest that:

- Training must explore various conceptions of literacy; participants' views of literacy acquisition must be made explicit. Training should also explore ways of connecting literacy instruction to issues of importance in learners' lives.
- Similarly, work with students should involve dialogue about their conceptions of literacy and their prior learning experiences; literacy instruction should incorporate culturally familiar literacy forms and practices, building on learners' oral language resources.

Why a participatory approach?

Adult learning theory

The view of literacy just outlined is congruent with recent perspectives from adult learning theory which suggest that adults learn best when instruction is contextualized in their life experiences, related to their real needs, and when they are involved in determining instructional goals and content. Their purposes for reading and writing can be expected to vary according to social contexts. Thus, adult learning theory, like literacy theory, suggests that the content of instruction should be linked to meaningful, authentic language and literacy use (rather than focusing on abstract, decontextualized decoding skills or generic topics). It must reflect students' everyday reality so that literacy becomes a tool that can enable learners to understand and change their lives (Kazemek, 1988; Knowles, 1984; Lytle, 1991; Nunan, 1988).

Curriculum theory

In order to implement this goal, the traditional concept of curriculum development must be changed; in the traditional model, the teacher identifies what is to be covered in a course (e.g., skills, grammar, competencies) before coming in contact with students; instruction then is a process of finding the most efficient way of transmitting this information from teacher to students. In place of this model, the concept of learner-centered and emergent curriculum development is becoming increasingly widespread. The new model involves collaborative discovery of learners' goals and concerns, involving constant dialogue and negotiation at every step of the way (Nunan, 1988). Chris Candlin (1984), a curriculum theorist, describes this as an interactive syllabus model

> which is social and problem-solving in orientation rather than one which transmits preselected and often predigested knowledge. The model thus becomes one in which participants, both teachers and learners, are encouraged to ask questions from the outset about syllabus objectives, content, methodology and experiences. (p. 34)

Adult ESL educators' practice

North American adult ESL educators have extended this learner-centered model to include content specifically focused on the social context of learners' lives, combining Freire's approach to literacy pedagogy with the emergent approach to ESL curriculum development (Auerbach, 1992; Barndt, 1987; Wallerstein, 1983). This participatory model for adult ESL literacy offers a systematic process for building curriculum around learners' lived experiences and social realities. As one of the Interns in our project said, in this model, "*The students' lives are the curriculum.*"

This participatory curriculum development process developed through this practice involves moving toward a model with the following components:

- **Investigation and identification of themes**: Teachers investigate the social conditions of learners' lives with them in order to identify their concerns and goals.
- **Re-presentation and dialogue**: As teachers discover what is important in learners' lives, they create or select materials to present the themes back to students as lesson content. Participants then discuss these issues in terms of how they have experienced them, their root or social causes, and possible strategies for addressing them.
- **Extension**: A range of tools are utilized to extend language and literacy proficiency, exploring these issues as the content of instruction. Materials and

learning activities (language experience stories, grammar and vocabulary work, reading and writing, role plays, etc.) focus on the issues.

- **Action**: Students apply what they have learned inside the classroom to address concerns outside the classroom.
- **Evaluation**: The class evaluates the learning process and the actions they have taken.

Of course, the challenge is adapting this model to particular groups of students. When the social context of learners' lives is incorporated in instruction, relevance is ensured. As students participate in identifying themes that are important to them, in developing learning tools they will use, and in evaluating what they have learned, they gain a measure of control over their own learning which extends to their lives outside the classroom.

. . .

Why literacy teachers from the communities of the learners?

The final feature of our project which fits with a social-contextual view of literacy and a participatory approach to adult education is its focus on training people from the communities of the learners as teachers. Although the idea of hiring teachers who do not have either traditional higher education or teaching credentials may seem unusual in the U.S. context, it is not uncommon in other parts of the world.

- In the early 1960s, a classic study of Spanish literacy acquisition among Mexican Indians found that learners taught by Indians from their own community with little pedagogical training learned to read in both the vernacular and in Spanish better than did those taught by native Spanish speakers from the dominant culture with more training (Modiano, 1968).
- Many of the mass literacy campaigns of third world countries are based on the principle that people who know a little more can teach people who know a little less. International organizations like UNESCO promote the strategy of relying on these nontraditional teachers as the main way of addressing widespread illiteracy.
- In Nicaragua, for example, it was the shortage of teachers that initially prompted the campaign to train people who had themselves just learned to read and write to become literacy workers. According to Fernando Cardenal (1990), the director of the literacy campaign and a poet, this decision

    came really out of the pressure of not knowing at that point exactly what to do. But we put our trust in the people and the extraordinary result was that it was incredibly successful and most of these people became very good teachers. In fact, the literacy workers' lack of traditional background was an advantage: they had shared the experiences of the learners and could say, "Look, I learned . . . so can you." The literacy workers' insecurity, lack of professionalism, and inexperience enabled them to be part of the students, helping them to overcome their fear of learning. (p. 45).

In the U.S., we would call this peer teaching; its power comes from the fact that barriers between teacher and learner are broken down.

Preliminary work in the United States suggests that this model is highly relevant for this context as well, and is particularly promising for adult native language literacy instruction. Beyond the fact that traditionally credentialed teachers may not be available (Anglo teachers may not be able to teach the L1 because they don't know it, whereas language minority teachers may opt for elementary or secondary positions because the pay is better), there are a number of reasons why community teachers are particularly suitable.

- In addition to sharing a linguistic background with learners, their shared cultural background can be a resource, enabling them to draw on culturally familiar discourse forms (e.g., fables, proverbs, rules for interaction).
- Their common cultural, political, and historical knowledge base can be integrated into learning.
- People from the communities of the learners are in a particularly good position to elicit and facilitate learning around learners' life experiences because they have shared them and can understand them. Their experience as immigrants or refugees, struggling with issues of transition to the new culture, can be a powerful tool for participatory curriculum development. Further, their own experience facing linguistic and cultural challenges enables them to act as role models for students and resources for colleagues trying to understand the issues facing language minority communities.

Several recent literacy programs and research projects provide evidence of the effectiveness of teachers from the learners' communities:

- D'Annunzio (1991) reports on a project in which Cambodians were trained to tutor ESL; he attributes much of its success to "the use of bilingual tutors who shared the students' experiences" and argues that, with brief training, bilinguals (who, in the case of this program, were "only high school graduates") can become effective tutors and trainers of other tutors. He concludes that this model "may break the chain of reliance on heavy professional intervention" (p. 52).

- Hornberger and Hardman's (1994) study of instructional practices in a Cambodian adult ESL class and a Puerto Rican GED class corroborates the importance of shared background between teachers and learners. In the case of the Cambodian class, they found that because the teacher herself was Cambodian, (1) the students had the option of using Khmer to respond to her questions and to help each other, (2) the teacher and students shared assumptions about the learning paradigm, and (3) classroom activities were intimately connected with learners' other life activities and cultural practices. Likewise, in the GED class, instructional activities were embedded in a cultural and institutional context that integrated and validated learners' Puerto Rican identity. Their study suggests that the reinforcement of cultural identity, made possible by the shared cultural background of learners and teachers, is critical not just for L1 literacy acquisition, but for ESL acquisition as well.
- Describing a project at the Quincy School Community Council in Boston's Chinatown, Hooper (1992) makes a powerful case for recruiting and training advanced ESL students as tutors for beginning learners. In his article, "Breaking the waiting list logjam: Training peer tutors for ESL," he reports that the project (called the Take and Give or TAG project) was designed in response to the fact that the program has over 1000 people on its waiting list who have to wait up to 4 years for a slot in the program. Students who have completed the highest level of ESL, but want to continue in the program and expand their ESL proficiency, are trained to provide home-based tutoring for students on the waiting list, utilizing a beginning ESL video series. According to Hooper, the fact that the tutor and the learner share a common first language and a common immigrant experience enhanced the model. Hooper claims TAG is working not only as an innovative solution to the waiting list logjam, but as a strategy for eradicating barriers to "empowerment, to personal and community resource development, and to self-direction and self-fulfillment . . . and to communication in English" (p. 4).

But what about the appropriateness of this model for ESL instruction? The notion that native speakers of English are the most qualified to teach ESL is almost axiomatic in TESOL circles. This notion rests on the assumption that linguistic competence is the single most important criteria for teaching and goes hand in hand with the assumption that English should be taught entirely monolingually. Increasingly, however, both of these assumptions are being challenged by researchers and practitioners.

Embedding literacy tuition within communities: a variety of approaches

As well as introducing literacy through learners' first languages, the Boston community project was based on a pedagogy of participation in the curriculum by the learners and the training of teachers from within the community (an approach shared with the El Barrio programme discussed in Chapter 3). However, bringing together a radical participatory approach, which focuses teaching around social issues, and the training and employment of teachers and teaching assistants from immigrant and refugee communities (called interns in this project), does create potential conflict, as Auerbach acknowledges:

> In some cases, Interns' prior educational experiences caused them to be uncomfortable with a participatory approach – they expected to teach and be taught in the ways they themselves had learned, which may have been quite traditional. Thus, some wanted the training to provide them with techniques and tended to rely on mechanical approaches in their own teaching. The rate and extent of change from a teacher- to a learner-centred approach was uneven. In addition, even when participants seemed very engaged in workshop activities, the extent to which they transferred workshop ideas to their own teaching was variable.
>
> (Auerbach, 1996, p. 156)

This observation takes us back to Bell's experience of Chinese literacy tuition, and the traditional approach taken by her tutor Lam, because that was how she was taught. In contrast, in the El Barrio programme discussed in Chapter 3, opposition towards new methodologies came from the learners, many of whom were expecting a more traditional teacher-fronted approach. Rivera says that the former students who were trained to become popular teachers on the programme are key to new students embracing change, since they become ardent advocates of the non-traditional methodology. Auerbach argues that, paradoxically, teachers are a central driving force in creating a participatory community: 'accepting one's power as a teacher entails enabling students to exert their power' (Auerbach, 2000, p. 147). For Auerbach, a teacher can be both a co-learner and a source of authority that encourages new ways of classroom learning.

Training language minority literacy teachers from the same communities as the learners means that both teacher and learners share cultural norms and practices. This common ground has also been used in programmes where only the additional literacy is taught. One example, observed by Hornberger, is a class of Cambodian immigrants being taught English language and literacy by a Cambodian teacher who had been in the USA since high school (Hornberger and Hardman, 1994) The learners' levels of literacy in Khmer were mixed. Most were literate despite little formal schooling, but some had no Khmer literacy. The teacher used formal teaching methods, which included copying and recitation of dialogues, distance between the students and teacher, and no use of Khmer when teaching. There was no attempt to contextualize the dialogues or vocabulary. The learners, on the other hand, behaved informally with each other. For instance, they used Khmer to help each other and, at times, brought their children into the class. Hornberger argues that the teacher and learners had created a context for learning that was appropriate to their desires and goals as language learners, even though literacy instruction was based on an autonomous view of literacy as a set of decontextualized cognitive skills. They were building a bridge to a new language through practices familiar to their first language and culture.

Drawing on community practices to foster literacy learning has developed differently in the Yemeni community of Sheffield in the UK. Although Yemeni families had lived and worked in Sheffield for up to twenty years, the majority had not needed English literacy for their employment in manufacturing jobs. The collapse of this sector, however, caused a great deal of unemployment in the Yemeni community in the 1980s. A literacy campaign was initiated, embedded within the community. Initially, twelve young unemployed Yemeni men and women aged between 18 and 26 were recruited for one year. They received training to support the English literacy learning of adult members of their community, and also attended special classes at a local university to provide them with an orientation towards academic studies (Gurnah, 2000).

Although the main focus of the campaign was English literacy for the older Yemenis, this tuition was part of a bilingual approach. Most of the older generations were literate in Modern Standard Arabic, whereas the younger generations could speak Yemeni Arabic but not write fluently. Therefore, the principle of exchange was established: the literacy assistants gave support in reading and writing English, and the older learners also had knowledge to impart to these younger community members. The campaign was sustained by the development of the Yemeni Economic and Training Centre, which was run by members of the community.

These different approaches show that there is not just one 'correct' way to teach an additional literacy. All of them, however, make room for the learners' culture and context of learning.

Discussion

1. Have you had any experience of learning to read and write a different writing system or script? If so, did you find your knowledge of your first literacy more of a help or a hindrance? If not, do you think ESOL literacy teachers should learn one as part of their professional development?

2. Auerbach, in Reading 3, defines the participatory approach as 'a systematic process for building curriculum around learners' lived experiences and social realities' (p. 121).

Is it possible, or even desirable, to establish a participatory model in:

- Classes where all the learners share language and culture?
- Classes where the learners come from diverse countries and cultures?
- A system where there is a centralized curriculum?

3. Why is it 'paradoxical' that teachers are a 'central driving force in creating a participatory community'? (See p. 125)

4. Bell, in Reading 2, says that 'ESL literacy teachers have to recognize that they are teaching more than the letters of the alphabet' (p. 115).

In your professional experience, have you found differences in learners' assumptions and beliefs about learning and being literate?

Research

What can you find out about a particular group of ESOL learners' use of reading and/or writing in their first languages outside the classroom?

How are these practices similar or different to their uses of reading and writing in English?

The Australian study of everyday reading practices briefly described in Chapter 2, pp. 52–53 (Burns and de Silva Joyce, 2000) would make a good model for this activity if you are able to get hold of the book.

Chapter 5

Learning the spoken language
From ideal to asymmetrical interaction

Introduction

In Reading 1, Ronald Carter refers to two orders of reality: the language studied and used inside the language classroom, and the language used to interact in different situations outside the classroom. We will explore some aspects of these two linguistic worlds in this chapter. First we will focus on some of the characteristics of spoken English that are used by English speakers in everyday contexts as revealed by analysis of data on computer corpora. We will compare these characteristics with representations of spoken English written especially for language learning in classrooms. We will then move back outside the classroom and look at research into how migrant workers in European countries actually manage to develop understandings of the spoken language in particular interactions with majority group speakers. Finally, we return to the classroom to consider tasks aimed at improving the grammatical accuracy of learners' speech.

Thus the discussion moves back and forth between these worlds inside and outside the classroom walls, just as ESOL learners move between the two. For language teachers the question is how to manage the relationship between these two orders so as to support the language development of learners.

'Real' spoken English

There now exist large data banks of both written and spoken English of all kinds. These are called computer corpora (one such bank is a corpus). The development of computer software has meant that detailed linguistic analysis of these collections may be carried out. As Reading 1 explains, the collection and analysis of large amounts of naturally occurring spoken English on one particular computer corpus demonstrate quite clearly that the rules of spoken English differ from those of the written language. I will start this chapter with a brief description of four features common to spoken English found from analysis of corpus data in order to illustrate this difference.

One of the most salient grammatical features of conversation is *ellipsis*, where some grammatical elements of an utterance which are not considered necessary for shared meaning making are left out (e.g. 'Told you so' (omission of 'I') or 'Understand?' (omission of 'do you')).

Another frequent feature of informal spoken English is the use of *tails*. This term refers to the position at the end of a clause which is available for extra information. This slot may be filled with a tag (e.g. 'Nice day, *isn't it?*' (notice also the ellipsis in this utterance)). Or the slot may be filled with a full noun phrase in order to extend or reinforce what the speaker is saying (e.g. 'It's actually not very good *that wine*' or 'They complain about it all the time *they do*').

Along with this kind of extension of a point through the use of tails, fixed phrases such as 'That's nice' or 'I thought so' often follow a question-and-answer sequence as a kind of interactional acknowledgement. Carter calls these *three-part exchanges*. They may be used to evaluate a response or demonstrate involvement in the interaction. These responses to answers do not carry much topical information but are part of the interpersonal element of any interaction, and Carter suggests that if they are not used, then the interaction may feel rather cold. Another way of signalling that one is listening is the use of *back-channelling*. Back-channels are often in the form of noises rather than words (e.g. 'Mm', 'Uhmn'). (For more details of the grammar of spoken English see Carter and McCarthy, 1997; McCarthy and Carter, 1995).

These are just some of the features that occur frequently in conversational English. Carter argues that these features are missing from dialogues in course materials whose function it is to teach the use of the spoken mode because these dialogues are frequently based on written English structures. In addition, 'real' spoken English is messy and untidy, he says, whereas the representations of spoken English in pedagogic materials are smooth, cooperative and problem-free. This makes the vocabulary and grammar much easier to understand and practice, and so suits the realities and purposes of the language classroom, but such language use does not mirror the language the learner will encounter outside the classroom.

Activity: Guided Reading

Reading 1:

Carter, R. (1998) 'Orders of reality: CANCODE, communication, and culture', *ELT Journal*, 52(1): 43–53.

It may be a good idea to read the article by Carter now. In it he questions the usefulness of the versions of spoken language often found in published classroom materials.

How relevant is his argument to the materials you have experience of?

This article is concerned with the topic of language awareness in relation to spoken texts and their cultural contexts. The topic has become more relevant in recent years, as we have witnessed the development of more and more corpora of spoken English; more exciting developments in the work of COBUILD; the growth of the British National Corpus, with its spoken components; and the development of CANCODE by the author and Michael McCarthy at Nottingham University, with the support of Cambridge University Press. The data in this paper are drawn from everyday situations of language use collected for CANCODE and developed with an eye to their potential relevance for ELT.

Real English

The CANCODE data is, of course, real data. Now 'real' is a word I'd like to dwell on for a moment because it is widely used at present in our cultures, particularly in our ELT culture. For example:

Real ale
Get real!
Enjoy that real country taste of Crackerbarrel cheese
You're out of touch with reality
Real English
Coca Cola . . . The Real Thing

The word 'real' invariably carries positive associations. People believe they want or are told to want or, indeed, *actually* want what is real, authentic, and natural in preference to what is unreal, inauthentic, and unnatural.

Three questions

Three significant concerns have emerged in the course of our research at Nottingham University. First, there are many features of real, naturally-occurring, spoken standard English grammar which are not recorded in the standard grammars of the English language. The major standard grammars are, of course, based largely on the written language and on examples drawn from single-sentence, sometimes concocted, written examples. This raises the first question: in the light of new evidence, should we make any changes to the grammar we teach? Second, all the data collected so far have been collected in specific cultural contexts, almost all involving native speakers of English. CANCODE is soon to be extended to include several other international varieties of English, but at present all the examples illustrate standard British spoken English and aspects of British English cultures. This raises the second question: do we want the native speaker as our model, particularly if it means that we have to take the native speaker's culture as well? Third, is there an automatic transfer from natural, real, corpus-based spoken English to the textbooks and pedagogies used for the teaching of English as a second or foreign language? In other words, and this raises the fourth question: in the light of all this new information, should we modify our teaching materials or not?

What can real spoken English reveal?

There is a focus in CANCODE on interpersonal communication in a range of social contexts and, wherever possible, differences and distinctions are drawn between the kinds of language used in those contexts. By providing many examples of English used in informal contexts, comparisons can be made which are of potential use to language teachers and learners, since they illustrate how speakers make different choices according to the situation they are in.

The key theoretical and practical concerns are not with general sociological categories but with specific language choices: which forms of language do we choose for which purposes, and which interpersonal choices do we make according to whom we are interacting with? The key issue for materials writers and teachers, therefore, is whether we can generate and teach materials which help learners to choose and interact appropriately, particularly along a continuum from written to spoken discourse.

Here are some examples of what CANCODE shows us about choices in the spoken language:

Three-part exchanges

Question and answer sequences in many real conversations are never simply questions and answers because they are accompanied by a follow-up move in which, in the third part, the questioner offers some kind of comment on or even evaluation of the answer:

    A: What part of London are you staying in?
    B: In Hyde Park.
    A: Oh, are you? That's a nice district.

    A: What time is it?
    B: A quarter past six.
    A: Is it? I thought it was later.
    (CANCODE)

The third part in such exchanges is regularly filled by what Lewis (1993) would call 'lexical chunks', that is, fixed or routinized phrases such as 'Really?', 'That's interesting', 'That's nice', 'I thought so', or 'I guessed as much'. Indeed, it is worth noting that the absence of a follow-up comment can make a question and answer sequence rather cold and impersonal. It is worth scrutinizing English language coursebooks to check whether there are more three-part than two-part exchanges. Our research at Nottingham University suggests that in some ELT materials and English language coursebooks, at least, two-part exchanges may be more common. (For further discussion see McCarthy and Carter 1994, Chapter 5: Tsui 1994.) However, in materials based on real English, such as the Collins *Cobuild English Course* (Willis and Willis 1988), we note that three-part exchanges are more common. Clearly there are issues here of a tension between truth to the language and pedagogic judgement. Or it may just be that you don't know these things about the spoken language until you collect real data.

Vague language

We are overwhelmed in our data by examples of what Channell (1994) has termed 'vague language'. Several English language coursebooks do not exhibit many examples of vague language, even though it is always pragmatically highly significant, and nearly always enables polite and non-threatening interaction. For example:

See you *around* six

Q: What time are we meeting?
A: Oh, seven-thirty or *thereabouts*.

There were *about* twenty *or so* people at the dinner.
(CANCODE)

In the case of time and number reference, vague language is non-authoritarian and puts speakers on an immediately casual and equal footing with their interlocutors. Comparison with utterances marked by their precision (e.g. 'See you at seven-twenty') reveals how much more formal and directive they are (see also Carter 1987).

Ellipsis

Ellipsis is one of the most frequent grammatical features found in our data, and its pervasive and endemic character is in inverse proportion to the sparse treatment it receives in many traditional grammars and course materials. (More detailed description is given in McCarthy and Carter 1995.) Preliminary exploration of data from other varieties of informal, spoken, international English reveals that ellipsis is also pervasive in these varieties.

Realities and coursebooks

In the examples below, real conversational data collected in a hairdressing salon (Example 1) is contrasted with an invented dialogue in a similar situation (Example 2), taken from a widely used and internationally renowned coursebook.

> Example 1
> [In the hair salon]
> **A**: Do you want to come over here?
> **B**: Right, thanks (3 secs) thank you.
> **A**: Tea or coffee?
> **B**: Can I have a tea, please?
> **A**: Do you want any sugar?
> **B**: Er, no milk or sugar, just black thanks.
> **C**: Right.
> **B**: I hate it when your hair just gets so, you know a bit long
> [**C**: Yeah] and it's just straggly.
> **C**: Right.
> **B**: It just gets to that in-between stage
> [**C**: Yeah] doesn't it where you think oh I just can't stand it any more (2 secs) I think when it's shorter it tends to, you notice it growing more anyway [**C**: Mm] you know it tends to grow all of a sudden . . .
> (CANCODE)

> Example 2
> [At the hairdresser's]
> **Jane**:   . . . Oh, yes, my husband's wonderful!
> **Sally**: Really? Is he?
> **Jane**:   Yes, he's big, strong, and handsome!
> **Sally**: Well, my husband isn't very big, or very strong . . . but he's very intelligent.
> **Jane**:   Intelligent?
> **Sally**: Yes, he can speak six languages.
> **Jane**:   Can he? Which languages can he speak?
> **Sally**: He can speak French, Spanish, Italian, German, Arabic and Japanese.
> **Jane**:   Oh! . . . My husband's very athletic.
> **Sally**: Athletic?

Jane: Yes, he can swim, ski, play football, cricket and rugby . . .

Sally: Can he cook?

Jane: Pardon?

Sally: Can your husband cook? My husband can't play sports . . . but he's an excellent cook.

Jane: Is he?

Sally: Yes, and he can sew, and iron . . . he's a very good husband.

Jane: Really? Is he English?

(Hartley and Viney, *Streamline English Departures*, Unit 14) (1978)

The real data in Example 1 contains features familiar to anyone who has scrutinized real English spoken discourse: a preponderance of discourse markers ('right' as an acknowledgement); ellipsis; the use of hedges (particularly the adverb 'just'); vague language ('you know', 'that in-between stage'); supposedly ungrammatical forms ('a tea'); as well as the use of 'tend to' to describe habitual or regular actions and events. ('Tend to' is one of the most frequent verbs in the CANCODE data, but while several of the standard grammars recognize its semi-modal status, they give more attention to the more central modals, and do not differentiate the verb's provenance in spoken compared to written discourse.)

Example 2 works well pedagogically. One of the main points of the exchange is to teach the modal verb 'can', and this point of presentation overrides other features of the situation. There is thus a further pedagogic reality to be noted: that in some successful coursebooks, rather than the dialogue taking precedence over the linguistic features to be learnt, the language teaching points take precedence over the reality of the dialogue. Many materials writers and teachers would say that in most circumstances such design features are inevitable. In other words, we should look at how much practice is given in this material, particularly in the posing and answering of questions, and in the use of the modal *can*, as well as at how much vocabulary is introduced and practised. In this respect, compare it to the real hair salon data, where the exchanges are natural but not lexically rich – as is common in informal conversations, the same words tend to be recycled, and the topics are seldom noted for their interesting content. In many classrooms, straggly hair which grows too quickly may have a limited topic life.

There are a number of general observations which can be made about the nature of interpersonal interaction in Example 1 which marks it off as naturally-occurring discourse. For example, speakers interrupt each other and speak at the same time. There are longish pauses, backchannelling, and the use of contentless utterances such as 'yeah', and 'Mm' which indicate that contact is being maintained, and serve to oil the wheels of the conversation; utterances are incomplete or are completed by the other speaker; and the conversation drifts along without any marked direction. By contrast, the language of some coursebooks represents a 'can do' society, in which interaction is generally smooth and problem-free, the speakers co-operate with each other politely, the conversation is neat, tidy, and predictable, utterances are almost as complete as sentences, no-one interrupts anyone else or speaks at the same time as anyone else, and the questions and answers are sequenced rather in the manner of a quiz show or court-room interrogation.

The two texts therefore represent different orders of reality. The scripted text is *unreal* English, which is unlikely to be reproduced in actual contexts of use but is easier to comprehend, and more real pedagogically; the unscripted text is *real* English, but more difficult to comprehend and to produce, and therefore likely to be considered less real pedagogically. It is worth scrutinizing the spoken materials we use in our teaching in the light of these poles of reality.

Here are two more samples of the corpus data, both taken from service encounters of the kind which are regularly reproduced in teaching materials.

Example 3
[In the post office]
A: Right, send that first class, please.
B: That one wants to go first class, right we'll see if it is, it's not 41, it's a 60, I thought it would be, I'd be in the . . . 60 pence . . . there we are.
A: Lovely, thank you.
B: Okay, 70 80 whoops 90 100.
A: Thanks very much.
B: Thank you.
(CANCODE)

Example 4
[In the post office]
A: Can I have a second class stamp, please.
B: You can . . . there we are.
A: Thank you.
B: And one penny.
A: That's for me to spend is it?
B: That's right.
A: I bought a new book of ten first class when I was in town today and I've left them at home in me shopping bag.
B: Have you?
A: And I've got one left.
B: Oh dear.
A: Bye.
B: Bye.
(CANCODE)

These data are interesting, in particular, for the number of exchanges which are interpersonal rather than simply transactional and informative. Examples 3 and 4, for instance, illustrate the extent to which the exchanges are three-part rather than two-part exchanges, and with a third part which is markedly interactive and affective in some way, sometimes to the point of inserting personal anecdotes, discourse markers, or non-propositional language ('whoops'). Notice again how the spoken grammar breaks the rules of textbook grammar ('Right, send that first class please'), in that real spoken standard English not infrequently combines politeness markers and imperatives. Or 'That one wants to go first class', when a modal verb is used ungrammatically (but, in spoken standard British English, perfectly normally) with a non-animate subject such as a parcel.

In Example 5, also a service encounter, the situation is markedly different:

Example 5
[In a fish and chip shop]
A: Can I have chips, beans, and a sausage?
B: Chips, beans, and a sausage.
A: Yeah.
B: Wrapped up?
A: Open, please.
(CANCODE)

In terms of speaking cultures, the data illustrate some of the possible dangers of real speech, which is often messy and untidy, and embedded deeply in cultural understandings of various kinds to the point where individual words and choices of grammatical form can be of considerable cultural significance. Notice here, for example, how the word 'open' becomes contextually constructed into an antonym of 'wrapped up', and carries a specific cultural meaning of food being served in paper so that it can be eaten immediately, even perhaps while walking home. How far should such allusions be removed, and how relevant is it to learn to make cultural observations of the kind that fish and chip shops in Britain are just as likely, if not more, to sell sausages, burgers, and curry with chips as they are to sell fish and chips?

The language of the fish and chip shop is mainly transactional and, in fact, anything more interactive and interpersonal would be out of place because there are normally long queues of hungry customers in the shop. We should note in this respect how appropriate the ellipsis is, and how in such circumstances the full forms would be unnecessarily elaborated and even long-winded. However, some coursebook exchanges employ full forms, on the perfectly realistic pedagogic premise that you cannot ellipt utterances until you know and have first practised the full forms from which the reductions are made. Having said that, ellipsis is not particularly pervasive, even in intermediate to more advanced coursebooks, and learners are rarely presented with opportunities to understand which choices of which alternative forms are appropriate for which communicative purposes.

Speaking cultures

One common feature of the CANCODE data is the large number of formulaic, fixed phrases that are used in spoken discourse. The findings again endorse the view expressed in Lewis (1993) that the language is made up of lexical chunks, and that language teaching and learning should give more systematic attention to such high profile features of the language. Many of the most fixed of fixed expressions are, of course, quite culture-bound. And learners who are taught to read and see through such language can learn quite a bit about the cultures in which the language is embedded.

For example, what can we learn about English culture from the following idioms and fixed phrases, all of which involve some reference to foreign, in this case mainly European, nations?

Dutch courage
to go Dutch
double-Dutch
Dutch cap
If that's true, then I'm a Dutchman
Dutch auction

It's all Greek to me
Beware of Greeks bearing gifts

French leave
French letter
French kiss
French lessons

Here we learn several useful and widely used phrases, but we can also learn something about British insularity, and that distrust of foreigners to the point where the British can be interpreted as believing almost all of them to be either unintelligible, untrustworthy, or 'unreal'. The phrases also reveal attitudes towards other languages than English, such as a feeling of linguistic superiority, and the suspicion that foreigners engage in sexual practices we dare not even mention, except by giving them a foreign name.

Other examples could, of course, be enumerated. One major issue here is the extent to which such cultural particulars are removed from data developed for purposes of classroom teaching and learning. It is argued below that such particulars can and should be retained in materials, provided a discovery-based language awareness component is used simultaneously to develop sensitivity to language and to enhance cultural understanding. Such skills are a not inessential component of 'seeing through', i.e. reading and learning how to interpret all cultural features and products, whether that culture be constructed with a small or a large 'c'. (See Brown 1990, Carter 1995, Carter and Nash 1990, Kramsch 1993.)

Conclusions

What conclusions can be drawn from the discussion so far?

1. On the one hand, we have real English which, as far as classroom treatment is concerned, can be unrealistic; and on the other hand, we have unreal textbook English which, as far as classroom treatment is concerned, is frequently handled in pedagogically viable and realistic ways.

2. Much spoken English is impregnated with cultural values. On the one hand, it is patronizing of teachers, coursebook writers, and materials designers to say to learners that we know what you should have and will therefore remove and neutralize all but the most accessible cultural reference. Is this realistic, when learners seem to want to know what real English is, and are generally fascinated by the culturally-embedded use of language of native speakers? Above all, learners know from their L1 experience when they are in the presence of concocted and culturally disinfected dialogues.

    On the other hand, we might want to argue that roughly 80 per cent of all spoken interaction in English is between non-native speakers, for example between a Turkish secretary and a Japanese supplier. For most learners, therefore, interactions with native speakers will be rare. It is surely unrealistic, and at the same time an imposition, to expect learners to acquire naturalistic, real, native-speaker English when they simply don't need it (Prodromou 1990, Rampton 1990, Phillipson 1992).

3. Those who argue that non-native speakers do not need exposure to real English assume that language learners only need to learn to transact, and have no real need to interact in the target language. On the other hand, it can be argued that, more often than is realized, language users at all levels also need to build relationships, express attitudes and affect, evaluate and comment, and make the propositional content of a message more person-oriented.

4. There are thus issues of power and empowerment at stake here. On the one hand, real English advantages and empowers the native-speaker-teacher, but disempowers the non-native speaker teacher. It is yet another version of cultural and linguistic hegemony. On the other hand, it would be clearly disempowering, and once again patronizing to teachers and learners, to say that we can ignore a lot of these informal and interactive meanings, because one

outcome would be to deprive the learner of pedagogic, linguistic, and cultural choices. Which strategy and ideology is the more disempowering?

Correctness and variable rules

It is, of course, misleading to suggest to learners of English that grammar is simply a matter of choices. Grammatical rules exist; they have been extensively codified, and form the core of the structure of (both spoken and written) language. Rules exist, for example, that prescribe that in Standard British English a plural subject has to be followed by a plural form of the verb, and that it is simply and unequivocally *incorrect* for us to write or say, therefore, that 'the buildings is very high'. Within a central core, choices are not possible.

As we have seen, however, there are areas of meaning which are selected within the grammar. Within the domain of spoken grammar we have also seen that it may be more accurate to speak in terms of variable rather than absolute rules for certain choices.

My own position is simply to say that teachers and learners can always choose *not* to teach and learn those areas of language where rules are more probabilistic than determinate, but that they have no choice at all if such options are not made available. Learners should not be patronized by being told that they do not need to bother with all this real English. They should not be disempowered, and syllabuses should not be deliberately impoverished. Also, learning a language should, in part at least, involve developing something of a 'feel' for that language. The folk-linguistic term 'feel' has been around for many years in language teaching, but it has remained a largely unanalysed concept. Learners who concentrate on the more rule-bound and referential domains are unlikely to develop the kind of sensitivity, personal response, and affect which probably underlies 'feel', and which goes some way to helping them discover, understand, and begin to internalize the expressive as well as the referential resources of a language.

Corpora of real, naturally-occurring English are not going to go away, and will become increasingly sophisticated and accessible. What are some possible solutions to these dichotomies? What might then be on our agenda as far as pedagogies for speaking Englishes and speaking cultures are concerned?

Pedagogies for speaking Englishes and speaking cultures

Language awareness

Recent research in the field of second language acquisition and development (Fotos 1994; Ellis 1991) has pointed to some advantages in procedures which raise learners' consciousness of particular grammatical forms. In spite of numerous pedagogic advantages, communicative teaching has not encouraged in students habits of observation, noticing, or conscious exploration of grammatical forms and function. In the case of the examples here such procedures may be especially appropriate, since we are attempting to introduce understanding of tendencies, variable rules, and choices according to context and interpersonal relations.

Thus, learners need to be made more aware of the differences in the use of different forms by exploring different Englishes in different contexts. Coursebooks might focus on particular learning priorities but also ensure that some opportunities are built in for students to learn to observe differences between coursebook and real English, preferably by focusing on passages with more or less the same content: for example, two dialogues in a hairdresser's shop or in a post office. We can all see, I am sure, a number of interesting ways in which modern communicative methodologies such as gap-filling, information gap, rewriting, and role play could help to enhance language awareness of the different grammatical choices, the different Englishes involved. Recent publications by McCarthy (1991), Nunan (1993), Bolitho and Tomlinson (1994), Brazil (1995), Woods (1995), and Van Lier (1995), in particular, offer a number of interesting possibilities, especially if the primary concern is with the development of reception and comprehension skills.

Text modification and modelling

Example 6 is a further illustration of the issues involved. It is a sample of data from CANCODE selected to illustrate tails in use. A is telling B what route he took in his car to get to B's house. Both A and B engage in a kind of phatic exchange, commenting on and reinforcing each other's remarks on the journey in a friendly, informal, and suitably interactive, interpersonal style. Repeated tails ('nice it was' and 'nice run that') figure prominently in the exchange:

> Example 6
> A: And I came over Mistham by the reservoirs, nice it was.
> B: Oh, by Mistham, over the top, nice run.
> A: Colours are pleasant, aren't they?
> B: Yeah.
> A: Nice run, that.
> (CANCODE)

One conclusion reached so far in the preparation of discourse grammar materials is that a middle ground between authentic and concocted data might be occupied which involves modelling data on authentic patterns. (See also McCarthy and

Carter 1994: 197–8.) Here is an example of a possible re-modelling of the data above:

A: And I came over by the village of Mistham. It was nice it was.
B: Oh, you came over the top by Mistham. That's a nice journey.
A: The colours are pleasant, aren't they?
B: Yes.
A: It was a nice journey that.

The attempt here by the materials developer is to achieve clarity, tidiness, and organization for purposes of learning, but at the same time to ensure that the dialogue is structured more authentically and naturalistically by modelling on real corpus-based English. It remains to be seen whether this is a weak compromise or a viable strategy. It could be argued that modelling data involves tampering with it to an extent that produces distortion; for example, if in the above data ellipsis is removed and difficult lexis and reference tidied up, then distortion may be introduced. Ellipsis may be a natural syntactic partner for tails structures (we do not yet know enough about such phenomena), and should therefore be retained. Similarly, tails and ellipsis may in turn sit more naturally alongside informal lexis such as 'run' (rather than 'journey'). At present research and materials development are continuing on the basis that text modification and modelling are viable strategies.

One interesting research possibility which may emerge from this process is a description of acceptable degrees of approximation to spoken English norms on the part of second and foreign language learners of English at different levels of development.

Understanding and misunderstanding in institutional discourse

The contrast Carter makes between the 'ideal' dialogues of course books and the 'real' messy and sometimes uncooperative conversations in life outside the classroom is supported by the findings of a research project funded by the European Science Foundation (ESF). This research tracked the informal language development of twenty-six migrant workers in five European countries over two and a half years in the 1980s. (This project was referred to in Chapter 1 in the section about language learning as socialization.) The informants in Germany, Sweden and France had received over a hundred hours of formal tuition in the majority language, but the rest of those studied had little or intermittent language instruction. After the end of the study some of the researchers involved carried out further analysis of the data collected from nineteen of the informants in order to identify and describe the processes of achieving understanding developed by the informants (Bremer *et al.*, 1996). The interactions focused on were between the minority ethnic workers and majority group members such as housing and employment officers. Reading 2 comprises case studies of two of the informants studied in this analysis.

The researchers in the ESF research originally aimed to collect naturally occurring data as they accompanied the informants in their daily lives. This proved to be difficult to achieve, so the final data were made up of some naturally occurring encounters, but also experimental tasks, simulated interactions, role-plays and feedback sessions with the informants. The simulated interactions were based around interviews with officials that all migrant workers have to cope with as they settle into a new country. These interviews are important for them, since they provide access to support services and training opportunities. In the feedback sessions, extracts from taped interactions were played back to the informant involved, who would then be invited to comment on anything of note. After the informant had made comments, the researchers would play the tape again and ask specific questions about seeming problems with understanding.

As a result, a detailed picture of the processes of achieving or not achieving understanding was built up. The analysis concentrated on the informants' reception of the spoken language. Whereas Carter, in the first reading, concentrates more on how we teach the production of the spoken language, these researchers argue that understanding is as important as speaking and that it is an interactive process, involving constant negotiation in interactions by participants. Their analysis showed that misunderstandings were caused by lack of linguistic knowledge on various levels. Problems could result from lack of understanding of particular words or phrases, or grammatical structure or the function of a discourse marker (that is, a word or phrase such as 'by the way', 'well', or 'however') by which a speaker gives information about what she is about to say. Lack of knowledge of the conventions of the interaction also led to misunderstandings (e.g. that it is 'normal' in European countries to discuss what kind of job you would really like to have in a job counselling interview), as did lack of cultural knowledge (e.g. the kinds of jobs available).

It is interesting to note that the use of ellipsis by the majority speaker often contributed towards misunderstandings, thus showing it is a common feature of institutional discourse as well as more informal interactions, and needs to be included in language teaching. The following extract from the research data provides an example of such a misunderstanding. It is from an interview between a Moroccan migrant to France, Abdelmalek (A), and a French lawyer (N). Abdelmalek had suffered a serious accident at work and was attempting to get compensation. In the interview he has just explained that, because of the accident, he had been unable to pay his rent and had been locked out of his room by the landlord.

> ○ *N:* Oui et alors *ça* en est *ou* pour l'instant
> [○ Yes and so *that's where* at the moment]
> ○ *A:* Euh ici a la première arrondissement
> [○ Here in the first district]
> ○ *N:* Non mais *la situation* elle en est a quel point
> [○ No but *the situation* it's got to what point]
>
> (Bremer *et al.*, 1996, p. 55)

As may be seen in the extract, the lawyer uses *ça* (that) elliptically to refer back to the incident with the landlord. He does not actually say 'the incident with the landlord', but that is what he means by *ça*. Abdelmalek does not understand what *ça* refers to and so guesses, from the subsequent use of *ou* (where), that this is a question about the geographical position of the room. His active hypothesis leads the lawyer into instant clarification as he replaces *that* with *the situation*.

Abdelmalek was one of the informants who was identified by the researchers as an active interactant, and thereby most likely to achieve successful communication. Overall, they identified the following strategies used to overcome misunderstandings:

- the use of metalinguistic comments on understanding and non-understanding, and attention to the linguistic items;
- initiative rather than dependency in their relationship to the majority partner in the interaction;
- a sensitive management of issues of face;
- an awareness of the issues in general.

(Bremer *et al.*, 1996, p. 105)

Learning the metalanguage of the majority language (that is, the language used to talk about language such as phrase, question, verb and so on) is part of the willingness of the informant to solve non-understanding and also develop their capacity to understand. The above extract shows Abdelmalek using the strategy of taking the initiative when processing an utterance that is difficult. Instead of just shaking his head or saying he does not understand, he makes a guess at the meaning of the question. Although it is not correct, it leads the lawyer to ask the same question in a different way (reformulation). In this way he also avoids saying directly that he does not understand, which can cause embarrassment or loss of face. The more advanced speakers of the new language used majority speakers' ways of signalling non-understanding and polite terms in order to avoid upsetting the majority speaker when interrupting.

📖   Activity: Guided Reading

Reading 2:

Bremer, K. *et al.* (1996) 'Case studies: the making of understanding in extended interactions', in Bremer *et al. Achieving Understanding: Discourse in Intercultural Encounters*, Harlow: Longman, pp. 110–117, 145–146, 151–154, 156–158.

In the extracts of case studies of Berta and Santo that make up Reading 2, there is more analysis of specific causes of misunderstanding and how the two informants try to overcome this.

What strategies do they use and how do they differ in their approach to achieving understanding?

5.1 Berta (Spanish–French): Job-centre Interview

+ difficile eh né pas de comprender *por por* français à + à travail de de cuisine
(+ *difficult eh not understand for for french at at work of kitchen*)

Berta came to France from Chile to follow her husband, a Chilean too, who had already been in the country as a political refugee for a year or so. Of course, she did not choose to emigrate to France. She is in her thirties and has had eight years of primary and secondary education in Chile. Without any professional training, she arrived a month before the project started and had no knowledge of French. She has three children, then aged seven to fourteen, who started to receive French schooling on arrival. For the first six months, the family lived in a refugee centre then they moved to a flat of their own in the Paris suburbs.

While still living in the centre, Berta seized the opportunity offered to her of working there as a replacement kitchen helper. But this was not a secure job and she was keen to better her social status. Her children were adapting rather well to French school life, and her friends and family, settled close to her (her mother had joined them in Paris for a while, her husband's sister had married a French man), provided a helpful environment. So she was getting ready to fight her way through the French world of work. This was her state of mind when she met the Job Centre counsellor. She was looking for an apartment and for a job and she knew she would have to fight. These interviews she had at that time, and the support of the people she met, reinforced her will to acquire some linguistic and professional competence, which she did later on.

However, at the time of the interview, Berta's competence in French was very limited since she had only been in France for seven months. But her life was changing. She had left the refugee centre and from then on she has had to take charge of everything: housing, living, job. The main interest she expressed in the interview (which took place at the unemployment office) was that she hoped very simply to find a regular job of whatever kind. The woman counsellor spoke very slowly but with long and complex utterances. She was very professional in the way that she strictly followed the standard script for a first interview, her questions aimed at the construction of a personal document of Berta. A strategy she used, very typical of these gatekeeping encounters, was to approach the different topics through indirect questions, which did not facilitate Berta's understanding.

Although, as a beginner, she had very few linguistic resources in French at her disposal, Berta was very willing to contribute to solving the understanding problems. This explains the high degree of commitment she kept maintaining during project interviews. She was also very much aware of problems of face and of the necessity to keep the interaction going smoothly. This combination resulted in a reduced use of direct signalling except for key misunderstandings (like the sequence on formation/information, see below). When she did not understand, she would rather signal her non-understanding by a minimal general query ('quoi?' what?). She even refrained from interrupting and would rather produce short minimal feedback utterances (hm) and let her partner continue or explicitly check on her comprehension.

At the same time, she tried to use her inferencing capacity and worked on forming hypotheses. Her limited linguistic means still prevented Berta from diagnosing her problem of understanding. So, the majority speaker made every possible effort to take this part of the joint work on herself. This explains the length of the diagnosis phase in some sequences.

The first third of the interview started with Berta's wishes and was centred on exploring the working conditions she was ready to accept: time, location, type of work. Then the counsellor turned to Berta's working and education experience (the second third of the interview) before testing her reaction regarding language and professional training and concluding on the necessity for Berta to be actively looking for a job herself (last third).

Wishing to present the partners' joint work in instances when understanding is difficult, we will analyse the main clarification sequences from different points of view:

the causes of the problem
the minority interactant's procedures in facing the problem
the majority locutor's complementary procedures and the type of collaboration.

The different sequences selected here focus on:

1.   a general failure in understanding,
2.   a problem in understanding solved by joint effort,
3.   a lengthy misunderstanding and its costly clarification.

The first excerpt that will be presented here is a good illustration of the
limitations of the possible exchanges when the minority interactant's resources
are very restricted and of the difficulties that are to be expected in such an
interaction, considering the topics, the diverging expectations and the discourse
style usually developed. The situation is as follows: after considering different
possible time schedules, the counsellor is trying to suggest to Berta that she might
have to travel far away from her home on the outskirts of Paris. Then she wants
to go into more detail, in particular she wants to check how far Berta is ready
to travel. The problem is that she approaches the matter through an indirect
and rather complex question which starts a rather frustrating sequence of non-
understanding:

N: d'accord + combien d'heures de transport vous pouvez faire par
     jour ↑
     ok + how many hours of travelling can you do every day ↑
B: quoi ↑
     what ↑
(120) N: combien d'heures + dans les transports en commun dans le métro ou
     dans le bus ↑
     *how many hours + on the public transport in the underground or on the
     bus* ↑
B: *por* metro ↑
     by underground ↑
N: oui combien d'heures I. vous pouvez faire ↑ ++ vous comprenez la
     question ↑
     yes how many hours can you do ↑ *you understand the question* ↑
B: (je) ne compris pas
     i do not understand
N: d'accord + alors dans paris je note hein dans paris
     ok + then in paris i write down ok in paris
(125) B: hm
N: ou proche de votre domicile
     or close to where you live
B: hm
     hm
N: près de chez vous + si c'est possible
     close to your home+ if possible

  B: euh *seis* + rue + *seis seis* + eh ↑ la *direccion* de moi ↑
    eh six + street + six six + eh? ↑ the address of me ↑
(130) N: non
    no
  B: non ↑
    no ↑
  N: vous accepteriez de travailler
    you would accept to work
  B: hm
    hm
  N: euh près de chez vous
    er close to your home
(135) B: hm
    hm
  N: près de font/à fontenay
    close to font/in fontenay
  B: hm
    hm
  N: ou alors + dans paris + mais pas à l'extérieur de paris
    or then + in paris + but not outside paris
  B: ah non *en el esterior de* paris non (rires)
    ah no in the outside of Paris no (laughs)
(140) N: d'accord ++ alors + bon maintenant vous allez m'expliquer ce que vous
    cherchez comme travail
    ok ++ then + well now you will explain to me what sort of work you
    want

This is a typical example of a failure in understanding, frustrating for both partners. Berta does not make any sense of the counsellor's question about transport (118) and is unable to link it with the problem of distance between workplace and home. The counsellor cannot go any further into her exploration of Berta's wishes and, finally, only makes a distinction between Paris and outside Paris and switches to the next topic.

 One must not forget that, compared to many other informants, Berta is a real beginner. This is why she accumulates difficulties in what is most of the time for her a global problem of understanding. Her linguistic repertoire is limited and the surface as well as the content of the counsellor's utterances are problematic, notwithstanding the pragmatic meaning. The only understanding approach available is for her to search for recognisable words. She herself explains, in the subsequent feedback interview, that she identified only two words from the counsellor's first utterance: combien (*how many*) and jour (*day*). And the difficulty is increased, as we would expect, by the indirectness of the question. Berta's minimal query: quoi? (what) indicates that she is at a complete loss concerning the surface topic of the new question presented to her. And, even more so, the covert topic (the distance from her home she is ready to travel for a job).

It is not the first time in the interview that the partners experience non-understanding. It has already happened twice when the counsellor has proposed some hypothetical situations as a means to get more precise indications on Berta's wishes and possibilities:

-et si on vous propose un travail plus tôt que huit heures ↑ vous accepteriez de le prendre ↑
and if you were offered a work earlier than eight o'clock ↑ would you accept it ↑

and

-et + vous accepteriez d'aller en banlieue ↑
and would you accept to go to the suburbs ↑

Hypothetical topics are a common source of non-understanding for minority interactants. Confronted with that type of question, they simply do not understand or take those questions for questions about the real situation. . . . In such a situation, Berta cannot even imagine that her preferences could be taken into consideration.

In the case we are analysing here, the counsellor, who tries to be helpful but does not diagnose the cause of Berta's non-understanding, reformulates in a way that is more explicit and more concrete. She offers specifications (public transportation) and common examples of Parisian means of transport in Paris (metro, bus)(120). But this is not enough for Berta to get the point. She manages to pick up one more word in the counsellor's reformulation (121: *por metro?*). Her reprise of the only word she has understood indicates that she needs more explication and help to figure out the counsellor's topic: acceptable distance for her to travel to work. This is why, considering that one more reformulation has got her nowhere, the counsellor decides to surface the problem and go on record (vous comprenez la question? *you understand the question?*). Berta answers clearly and explicitly, taking up her partner's words: no compris pas *I don't understand* (123).

Ratifying Berta's acknowledgement of non-understanding, the counsellor turns to her usual procedure of making a fresh start, summing up step by step what they have agreed on till then. Berta who feels very awkward not being able to understand after the question has been formulated several times chooses not to be explicit about her degree of understanding and sticks to minimal feedback. But, as the reformulation progresses, she feels she has to make a move towards elaborating meaning. Unfortunately, the new words used in the place of the proper names proposed first by the counsellor bring up another understanding problem. Berta who does her best to make inferences catches the word *domicile* ('home' in an official context), and turns to hypothesis forming. She starts an answer based on the plausible hypothesis that the counsellor is asking for her address. But, probably warned by the non-verbal symptoms produced by the majority speaker, she shies back and checks her hypothesis. She was right to be uncertain: the counsellor confirms that her hypothesis was wrong.

Partly aware of the cause of misunderstanding, the counsellor reformulates again keeping the hypothetical form (a conditional) which Berta is unable to grasp but also using proper names: Fontenay and Paris. And this gets them back to the more general agreement they had reached earlier. But the counsellor does not pursue any further. Considering the difficulty caused by this step backwards and willing to save both their energies for the rest of the interview after this partial failure, the counsellor ratifies and proceeds to the next topic.

The following excerpt bears on Berta's actual working experience. This time, Berta is so involved and she engages so much in the joint effort that she succeeds in overcoming another understanding problem. For this, she again has to draw inferences from the counsellor's very general question on what she does:

(180) N: ah ah d'accord et là qu'est-ce que vous faites alors ↑
           ah ah ok and there what do you do then ↑

       B: qu'est-ce que tu / eh la personne *del* chef* que el* m'explique + *el*
           m'explique eh que je prepare de manger
           *what do you / eh the person of the head who he explains to me + he explains
           to me eh what i prepare to eat*

       N: eh c'est / vous faites le menu avec elle ↑ ou
           eh it is / you do the menu with her ↑ or

       B: elle me dit *el* manger que *yo* préparé
           he/she tell to me the meal that i prepare

       N: hm et donc vous euh vous faites quoi dans la cuisine ↑ vous faites les
           achats aussi ↑ non
           hm and then you eh you do what in the kitchen ↑ you do the buying too ↑ no

(185) B: oui

       N: vous allez acheter ↑
           you go buying ↑

       B: oui + eh *por* trois mois solament
           yes + eh for three months only

       N: vous achetez pour trois mois ↑
           you shop/buy for three months ↑

       B: oui hm aujour/eh aujourd'hui + de septem/septembre à à décembre je
           trav(aille)
           yes hm to/eh to-day + from septem/september to december i wor(k)

190   N: ah ↑ vous travaillez d'accord pour trois mois
            ah ↑ you work ok for three months
      B: oui *por* trois mois
            yes for three months

This time again Berta is confronted with one of the counsellor's indirect questions and she has to infer her interlocutor's intention. The counsellor wants to know about her qualifications and the degree of responsibility Berta has in her cooking job. But Berta does not understand her point and first responds to the surface meaning of the question, describing very concretely what she does at her working place. And then, thinking her answer is satisfactory, she shifts topics and, as she holds the floor, she makes sure that the counsellor has understood that she really needs another job reminding her that this one is temporary (187: *por* trois mois solament). The counsellor has not followed her line and, still expecting her to give details on her qualification as a cook, she misinterprets, before rapidly rejecting such an irrelevant interpretation, Berta's remark (188: vous achetez pour trois mois?), helped in this by Berta's explanations (189: de septembre, à decembre je travaille).

. . .

5.4 Santo (Italian–English)

Santa was in his early twenties when he moved to London to join his English-speaking Italian girlfriend ten months before the start of the project. He had been to 'scuola media' in Italy, making a total of eight years of education, and after that he had worked in the catering trade in his home city, Naples, and on ships. He came from a large family of eleven children of which he was the fifth.

On arrival in England Santo found himself accommodation in a bedsitting room in suburbia near to where his girlfriend's family lived. He found employment in the centre of London. The job he held for the duration of the project was a chef's assistant in a restaurant in the City. The other workers in the restaurant came from other countries in Europe and South America. No one was a native speaker of English. However, Santo's contact with English was not as limited as some other workers in similar situations. He spoke some English with his girlfriend, talked to the other tenants in the house he lived in and went out to pubs and the cinema. Because of these contacts he did not give the impression of being isolated in any way. Although he was someone who evidently enjoyed communicating and who enjoyed the data collection sessions of the project, occasionally even going out voluntarily to record conversations and day-to-day interactions, he did not attend any language classes. This was not for lack of motivation to learn the language but, as for so many others in his position, there was little real opportunity given the nature of his work and the long hours spent in the restaurant. Unlike some other informants, he did not have children, and so there was no added incentive to learn in order to increase his career prospects or provide a better chance for the next generation. If anything, his girlfriend, with whom he finally returned to Italy, was more interested in encouraging their joint return rather than remaining in London. Of his own volition, Santo returned to Naples whenever possible, that is at Christmas and in the summer holidays, to visit his parents and siblings whom he was helping to support financially through his employment in London.

From the outset, Santo was one of the most outgoing and lively of the Italian informants. He appeared to be very confident and frequently initiated conversations with the researchers as well as taking the lead in guided tours. He frequently chose to keep to the conversation goals he had set himself and combined this with good interpersonal skills. Even in gatekeeping situations, he would attempt to create an atmosphere of joviality which sometimes misfired but which was generally taken as good humour. As the project data has shown, learners who themselves set the agenda as far as subject matter is concerned display fewer difficulties with understanding. Santo was certainly quite masterful in controlling conversations. By nature he appeared to be a *raconteur* and thus often wrested control of the topic away from his interlocutors. It is on this assertiveness that we focus.

. . .

Santo's assertiveness comes into play at several points in the encounter we have chosen to examine in detail which took place in an estate agent's office. During the actual recording, the estate agent was not aware of being recorded as she talked. Santo was accompanied by the Italian-speaking researcher on the project and occasionally addressed remarks to her in Italian, thus giving the impression that she was a friend accompanying him.

Although Santo was not seriously considering house purchase at the time of the recording, he had mentioned it as a possible option were he to stay in England. The encounter at the estate agent's is different from many other situations in which the minority speaker usually interacts because the power imbalance is not so heavily weighted towards the majority speaker. This is because the client goes to an estate agent voluntarily and, as a potential buyer, has to be courted. The client of course needs somewhere to live but there is a degree of customer control that would be unthinkable in the case of an applicant for council housing or for privately rented accommodation. The estate agent's aims are to provide a service. She wishes to match the client's interest and means as closely as possible to the property she has available and to provide the client with details of any property that might be considered suitable.

Santo opens the interview by stating his wishes and then waiting for the agent to respond with further questions or information, a strategy that, as Gumperz and Roberts (1991) point out, is common to many interethnic encounters.

(1) S: i want to buy + the house
      A: yes
      S: maybe three bedroom
      A: three bedrooms
(5) S: yeah
      A: erm what/roughly what price were you thinking of paying for the house
      S: forty thousand ↑
      A: forty ↑
(10) S: max yeah
      A: yeah erm i haven't got any houses around forty thousand for sale i don't
           think erm. i'll give you our list
      S: yeah what you think ↑
(15) A: that goes up to fifty i think (xxx) in the area that we cover erm for forty
           thousand you/it'd probably be a flat
      S: not a house ↑
      A: yeah you want a house though, do you ↑
      S: yeah a house
(20) A: yeah i haven't got any houses around forty erm + you see, around <here>
           it's quite expensive
           <indicating on the map>
      S: <islington>
           <reading>
      A: yeah whoops <low aside>
      S: too small this one
      A: yeah erm you see, we're here
(25) S: in islington is possible three bedrooms for forty thousand ↑
      A: two bedrooms ↑
      S: three
      A: well you might get a/perhaps a flat a large, but not round here for forty
           thousand erm you've got to go further north
(30) S: oh
      A: perhaps say towards <tottenham or somewhere up there>
           <points to map>
      A: you'd get i think you'd get a house there for about thirty five forty
           thousand but that's
      S: too long
(35) A: yeah i mean there is a tube station out there if you want to get into london
           central london quite easily
      S: <seven sisters>
           <reading the name of the tube station on the map>
      A: yeah but erm i think you'll find it very difficult to get at you/to get a

three-bedroomed house for forty thousand we just haven't got anything
like that

(40) S: (xx) how much you think it cost for three bedroom ↑

A: three bedroom ↑

S: fifty ↑

A: er + erm depends where + if it's around here then [it would probably be]
about seventy between seventy

(45) S: [in this area]

A: and seventy five if you go out say to stoke newington around <here>
<indicates on map>

S: mm

(50) A: then you might get one for about fifty + sixty + or say forty eight sixty
something like that

S: very expensive area anyway

A: well this this is expensive this is less expensive

By (52) Santo demonstrates agreement with the agent's assessment of the situation. This agreement has been an extended process and demonstrates Santo's ability as a learner to pursue his own goals, even though the majority speaker he is interacting with may not share his aims and has, in this case, already signalled very firmly that she does not believe that they have any property on her books that would meet Santo's requirements. The implied message behind 'i'll give you our list' (12) is, then, an indication that Santo should go away and use the detailed information on the list to realise that it is impossible to find a house at the price he wants in the area he wants. It is a pre-closing statement and it could, and probably would, be perceived by a majority speaker as an invitation to leave. Santo, however, does not (choose to) hear this and engages the estate agent with his next question which constitutes the start of a long process of familiarising himself with the variables of buying property in this part of London.

What is established next, then, at (15) is that for £40,000 one might find a flat but not a house in that part of London. Santo then checks back quite explicitly at (16) with 'not a house ↑' which prompts the agent in turn to confirm that Santo is indeed looking for a house. There is then a re-run of the same information until (28) where the agent makes her earlier statement 'not . . . around here' more particular by specifying 'you've got to go further north . . . perhaps say towards tottenham'. This information, combined with the following utterance, 'i think you'd get a house there for about thirty five forty thousand', makes it clear to Santo where the boundaries of expensive and less expensive property lie in this part of London. What has now been established for him is:

1.   he can't buy a house, only a flat, for the price he wishes to pay in the Finsbury
     Park area

2. he might find a house for that price, but it would be further north, around Tottenham.

The statements by the agent at (16), (29) and (31) all indicate that really Santo is looking for property in the wrong location. On none of these occasions does Santo acknowledge the possible closing force of these utterances and instead pursues his own goals of refining his knowledge of the property market. The topic moves on to Santo's need for ease of access to public transport into the centre of London:

      S: too long
(35) A: yeah i mean there is a tube station out there if you want to get into london central london quite easily
      S: <seven sisters>
      A: yeah but erm i think you'll find it very difficult to get at you/to get a three-bedroomed house for forty thousand we just haven't got anything like that
(40) S: (xx) how much you think it cost for three bedroom ↑
      A: three bedroom ↑
      S: fifty
      A: er + erm depends where + if it's around here then [it would probably be] about seventy between seventy
(45) S: [in this area]
      A: and seventy five if you go out to say stoke newington around <here> <indicates on map>
      S: mm
(50) A: then you might get one for about fifty + sixty +or say forty eight sixty something like that
      S: very expensive area anyway

This shift is very typical of the way in which Santo frequently conducts conversations, and in this interaction, it is a method of maintaining involvement even when the agent evidently feels that she cannot meet Santo's demands.

. . .

Santo's refusal in this encounter to let the agent set the agenda is interesting from two perspectives. The first is concerned with why Santo chose to resist the agent's attempts at closure. We can only surmise that it could be one or a combination of many factors that include the wish to please the researchers by getting more data, or real lack of understanding on Santo's part that the agent was trying to close the encounter, or his wish to establish what the parameters to house purchase really were. The second is concerned with the behaviour of the majority speaker: what was it that prevented the estate agent from showing exasperation or impatience towards Santo openly? One possibility is that politeness constraints prevented the agent from being any more explicit than she was, although the cumulative force of her comments would be sufficient for any majority speaker to terminate the interaction at a much earlier stage. Another explanation lies in a feature of Santo's interactional skills which he brings to bear in this encounter and which he consistently displays in many others, namely, his ability to maintain conversational involvement.

There are two ways in which Santo manages to keep the conversation going. The first is to ask questions that will elicit expert advice at points at which it looks as if the interaction is about to grind to a halt. There are examples of this at (14), (40) and (110) and each time the estate agent is persuaded into proffering more advice.

The second feature of Santo's interactional style that appears to work in his favour is that he volunteers comments that induce further suggestions and advice from the agent. Two examples of this occur during the discussion about travelling time and transport at (79) and again at (87).

> A: take you twenty five minutes i suppose twenty minutes twenty five minutes
> S: anyway for er forty thousand very complication yeah youve got er
> (80) A: very difficult + erm even two bedroomed flats is not too easy now
> S: no
> A: erm + i think if you want a house and you want three bedrooms you have to go and call at the agents' out this way more/
> S: seven sisters
> A: round tottenham, seven sisters yes
>   <i no like this area for me>
>   <laughing>
> A: you might errm if you go s bit further north you might get something out here with three bedroom i've got a house
> (90) S: in this area ↑

Such a feature contributes to the ease of his conversational style since it takes account of the unspoken needs of a conversation partner to remain engaged in the topic and has the advantage of triggering new information from the agent.

Throughout the project, Santo used his interactional skills in order to obtain the information he needed. At times, it is not clear whether he had understood or not. Most majority speakers chose to assume that he had, and not to embark on a clarification process with its accompanying risks. For such a learner who appeared to have good interactional skills, it is puzzling that by the end of the project Santo had not acquired more English than he did.

There are several possible reasons for this. It may be that Santo lacked the very strong motivation necessary to improve his English; his personal circumstances did not demand acquisition. He also lacked the physical opportunity to learn because of his long working hours. Another possibility, and one for which there is some evidence, is that he was so intent on achieving his own particular conversational goals that he sometimes appeared to disregard the contributions that his conversational partner made or certainly did not use them as part of an active learning process. ... Repeated behaviour of this kind could be interpreted as evidence of being a poor listener and could thus have a negative effect on the majority speaker's willingness to participate as well as Santo's own readiness to engage.

Nonetheless, through Santo's interactions we have evidence of a learner who uses his assertiveness to redress the imbalance of power between minority and majority speaker and yet who manages to do so in most situations in such a way that neither he nor his conversational partner loses face in the process.

We can see from the analyses of the conversations that Berta and Santo approached the tasks of understanding the person they were talking to in very different ways. The authors described Berta as 'an active and willing partner. Her contribution to the construction of understanding is strategic' (Bremer *et al.*, 1996, p. 123). Two of these strategies were to use unspecific words like 'quoi?' to signal a general misunderstanding, and hypothesis-forming. She became a successful learner of French. Santo, on the other hand, attempted to avoid misunderstandings by controlling the conversation, and smoothed over awkward communication by changing the topic or contributing an evaluative phrase.

The good language learner revisited

The active interactants who used strategies such as those listed above may certainly be described as 'good language learners' as discussed in Chapter 2 of this volume. In fact, the findings of this research could be said to match the ethnographic study of migrant workers in Canada as carried out by Norton (Chapter 2, Reading 2). It seems probable that Eva, the successful language learner identified by Norton, would have used many of the strategies for understanding listed by Bremer *et al.* The informants identified as less successful in the ESF research tended to rely on indirect feedback and to allow the majority language interactant to do the work of checking, diagnosing and repairing misunderstanding. In this way it is argued that they avoided the face-threatening act of interruption, but often failed to achieve successful communication.

However, both Bremer *et al.*, and Norton argue that the reasons that some of their informants were more successful language learners than others are complex, and cannot be attributed solely to the use of a particular set of strategies. Both studies found that most of the informants had very restricted opportunities to actually use the majority language at all, except within the kind of institutional interactions described in the case studies, where there is usually very little equality between the migrant worker and the speaker of the majority language. Indeed,

Norton argued that it was Eva's ability to gain access to the social networks of English speakers that resulted in her proficiency in the language. Similarly, the ESF research collected ethnographic data on the informants which showed them struggling not only with a new language, but also with difficult physical conditions and long hours at work, or complex domestic situations. For example, two of the informants were young Turkish workers in Germany. Both received combined language and skills training. Both found labouring jobs. But one enjoyed a good relationship with his supervisor, whereas the other had direct experience of racial discrimination that caused rejection, limited interaction and little development in the new language.

These studies show yet again the complex relationships between language acquisition and the social environment. The ESF data also show that there is no straightforward relationship between the management of understanding and becoming a proficient speaker in the additional language, as we explore in the following section.

Developing accuracy in the spoken language

The analysis by Bremer *et al.* shows some of the processes of achieving understanding in interactions in an additional language. These processes involve speaking as well as listening, as the more successful informants signal their misunderstandings and try to manage interruptions or communication problems in a non-threatening way. Santo, an Italian migrant in London, whose case study forms part of Reading 2, is another example of an active interactant. Santo nearly always manages to get the information he needs, despite misunderstandings, by asking questions and volunteering comments. Extracts from his interactions show that he is familiar with the three-part exchanges described at the beginning of this chapter, for example. However, by the end of the research period his spoken English was still extremely inaccurate and the researchers felt he had made little progress in extending his proficiency in speaking.

Santo's case bears similarity to that of Wes, a Japanese learner of English in Hawaii whose English acquisition in informal settings was the focus of a sociolinguistic study over two years (Skehan, 2001). According to this study Wes was not interested in instruction or using accurate grammatical structures, but wanted to be able to communicate with other people. By the end of the two years of the study it is reported that he had achieved his goal, as he had succeeded in being regarded as an acceptable conversation partner. He could take part in conversations in a more fluent and relaxed way, but his speech remained full of grammatical inaccuracies.

Learners like Santo and Wes are not uncommon. They achieve fluency and demonstrate good communication skills, but their knowledge and use of grammar stays undeveloped. Their spoken language is full of errors and deviant forms of the additional language. These have sometimes been called 'fossilized' errors by researchers as they seem to be impervious to change.

These two case studies suggest that this lack of spoken language development may have a variety of causes. Whereas Wes was simply not interested in developing grammatical knowledge, there is no record of Santo's attitudes towards language learning. His opportunities to improve his linguistic knowledge were limited, since he worked very long hours and did not have the opportunity to go to language classes. It was also noted by the researchers that, in the recorded interactions, he was sometimes so intent on achieving his aim that he did not always take notice of what the other participant was saying. This could indicate, they suggest, that he is a poor listener.

If we go back to theories of language acquisition discussed in Chapter 1, especially the theory that learners must notice the gap between their own language use and the 'input' in order to develop their interlanguage, then those learners who are poor listeners are unlikely to notice the 'gap' between their language use and those of the person they are talking to. It is suggested that one way language teachers can help such learners improve the accuracy of their speech is to carry out tasks in the classroom that promote 'noticing', as well as provide information about the language that may be drawn upon by the learner.

Research into the design and efficacy of such tasks was carried out by Sally Bird with four learners from an ESOL class she was teaching in London (Bird, 1998). One of these learners had been in the UK for some time and had achieved fluency, but, like Santo and Wes, her use of grammatical structures remained undeveloped. Bird put the learners into two pairs and tape-recorded them as they carried out a communicative task. She then listened to the tape and made a note of errors. She then played the tape to the learners and asked them to listen and stop the tape when they identified a problem. She then played the tape again and identified and discussed inaccuracies not noticed by the learners. They then repeated the communicative task. This procedure was carried out a number of times. Bird reports that when the learners repeated the task they did indeed incorporate the modifications discussed with her, and demonstrated awareness of the importance of grammatical accuracy. However, they found it difficult to notice their own inaccuracies on the first playing of taped tasks and relied heavily on the teacher for this. The transfer from teacher monitoring to self-monitoring was a slow process.

Obviously, such a teacher-centred set of tasks would not be suitable for a regular language classroom. However, Scott Thornbury argues that many awareness-raising classroom activities may be adapted for the promotion of noticing (Thornbury, 1997). He points out, for example, that the key method of a particular approach to language teaching called Community Language Learning (CLL) may be modified to promote noticing, as it is based on the reformulation of the spoken language. In CLL students sit in a closed circle around a tape-recorder and record a conversation of their choosing on to the tape. The teacher stays outside the circle and is available, on request by any learner, to help formulate what any learner wants to say. At the end of the conversation the tape is played through and is then transcribed (by teacher or students) on to a whiteboard or transparency. To promote noticing, Thornbury suggests that this activity could be carried out without any support by the teacher during the initial conversation, allowing opportunity for errors in the conversation to be noticed and discussed by the learners once it is transcribed.

Bridging two worlds

Of course, classroom tasks such as those described above do not take into account the power imbalance of interactions which are so often a large part of ESOL learners' experience of English outside the classroom. In such interactions, minority language speakers have to convey complex information with limited additional language proficiency, and they also often have to do so in uncomfortable and sometimes racist encounters. The dialogues and conversations in language-teaching materials usually differ from such reality not only in terms of linguistic structures, as Carter argues; they also avoid representations of uncooperative or unequal interactions. An important issue in language teaching is how the ESOL classroom may be used to support the learners to communicate effectively in the complex and sometimes unfriendly world beyond the classroom doors.

Discussion

1. In Reading 1, Carter suggests that interactions recorded for computer corpora should be tidied up a little and used in the classroom in place of the ideal dialogues of course books. Cook, however, in a response to Carter's article, defends the principle of invented dialogue as follows:

   Something is not a good model simply because it occurs frequently. A good deal of actual language use is inarticulate, impoverished, and inexpressive. Inevitably, because one cannot teach everything, part of the job of teachers and course designers is to select the language use which they wish their students to emulate. Many foreign language students have strong feelings about this too. They do not want to learn just any English because it occurs in a corpus, and it is patronising to overrule them. . . .

   To be corpus driven, in short, deprives everyone (native and non-native speaker alike) of the opportunity for choice and to make their own impact on the language.

   (Cook, 1998, p. 61)

   Should classroom tasks for ESOL learners be based on 'real' or 'ideal' interactions?

   What 'English' do your students want to learn?

2. What can we learn about the processes of learning to understand and speak an additional language from the case studies of Berta and Santo?

Research

Select a dialogue from a textbook or materials you have been using in the classroom. Explore the language use by looking for the following features:

- Ellipsis
- Tails
- Three-part exchanges
- Vague language

Would you describe the dialogue as 'concocted and culturally disinfected' (Carter, 1998, p. 50)?

You could extend this activity by comparing the textbook conversation with a 'real' one in a similar setting. To do this you would need either to record an encounter yourself, or search for one already transcribed and published in research materials or data banks.

References

Chapter 1

Bremer, K., Roberts, C., Vasseur, M-T., Simonot, M. and Broeder, P. (1996) *Achieving Understanding: Discourse in Intercultural Encounters*. Harlow, Essex: Longman.

Candlin, C. and Mercer, N. (eds) (2001) *English Language Teaching in its Social Context*. London, Routledge.

Ellis, R. (2001) 'Non-reciprocal tasks, comprehension and second language acquisition', in M. Bygate, P. Skehan and M. Swain (eds). *Researching Pedagogic Tasks: Second Language Learning, Teaching and Testing*. Harlow, Essex: Pearson Education.

Firth, A. and Wagner, J. (1997) 'On discourse, communication, and (some) fundamental concepts in SLA research'. *The Modern Language Journal*, 81, pp. 285–300.

Johnson, K. (1996) *Language Teaching and Skill Learning*. Oxford: Blackwell.

Krashen, S. (1985) *The Input Hypothesis*. London: Longman.

Long, M. (1988) 'Instructed interlanguage development', in L. Beebe (ed.) *Issues in Second Language Acquisition: Multiple Perspectives*. New York: Newbury House.

Lyster, R. and Ranta, L. (1997) 'Corrective feedback and learner uptake: negotiation of form in communicative classrooms'. *Studies in Second Language Acquisition*, 19, pp. 37–61.

McLaughlin, B. (1987) *Theories of Second Language Acquisition*. London: Edward Arnold.

Mitchell, R. and Myles, F. (2001) 'Second language learning: key concepts and issues', in C. Candlin and N. Mercer (eds) *English Language Teaching in its Social Context* London: Routledge.

Skehan, P. (2001) 'Comprehension and production strategies in language learning', in C. Candlin and N. Mercer (eds) *English Language Teaching in its Social Context*. London: Routledge.

Slimani, A. (2001) 'Evaluation of classroom interaction', in C. Candlin and N. Mercer (eds) *English Language Teaching in its Social Context*. Cambridge: Cambridge University Press.

Swain, M. (1995) 'Three functions of output in second language learning', in G. Cook and B. Seidhofer (eds) *Principles and Practice in Applied Linguistics*. Oxford: Oxford University Press.

Swain, M. and Lapkin, S. (1982) *Evaluating Bilingual Education: A Canadian Case Study*. Clevedon, Avon: Multilingual Matters.

Chapter 2

Allwright, D. and Bailey, K. (1991) *Focus on the Language Classroom: An Introduction to Classroom Research for Language Teachers*, Cambridge: Cambridge University Press.

Burns, A. and de Silva Joyce, H. (eds) (2000) *Teachers' Voices 5: A New Look at Reading Practices*, Sydney: National Center for English Language Teaching and Research, Macquarie University.

Carlson, M., Gustafsson, B., Lodeiro, E., Pedersen, A. and Kirchhoff, S. (2001) *Helhetssyn, professionalism och kontinuitet: en utvardering av arbete med sfi-studerande med posttraumatiskt stressyndrom*, Goteborg, Sweden: Annedals vuxengymnasium.

Ellis, R. (2001) 'The metaphorical constructions of second language learners', in M. Breen (ed.) *Learner Contributions to Language Learning*, Harlow, Essex: Longman.

Horsman, J. (2001) *Too Scared to Learn: Women, Violence and Education*, Mahwah, NJ: Lawrence Erlbaum Associates.

Kegan, R., Broderick, M., Drago-Severson, E., Helsing, D., Popp, N. and Portnow, K. (2001) *Toward a New Pluralism in ABE/ESOL Classrooms: Teaching to Multiple 'Cultures of Mind'*, Boston, MA: NCSALL.

Khanna, A., Verma, M., Agnihotri, R. and Sinha, S. (1998) 'Teacher evaluation of Asian ESOL learners in Britain and its social psychological correlates', in R. Agnihotri, A. Khanna and I. Sachdev (eds) *Social Psychological Perspectives on Second Language Learning*, New Delhi: Sage.

Langer, J. (ed.) (2002) *Crossing the Border: Voices of Refugee and Exiled Women*, Nottingham: Five Leaves Publications.

Larsen-Freeman, D. (2001) 'Individual cognitive/affective learner contributions and differential success in second language acquisition' in M. Breen (ed.) *Learner Contributions to Language Learning: New Directions in Research*, Harlow: Pearson Education.

Norton, B. (2000) *Identity and Language Learning: Gender, Ethnicity and Educational Change*, London: Longman/Pearson Education.

Roden, J. (1999) 'Swedish as a second language project for refugees'. *Language Issues*, 11: 8–10.

Sunderland, H., Klein, C., Savinson, R. and Partridge, T. (1997) *Dyslexia and the Bilingual Learner: Assessing and Teaching Adults and Young People who speak English as an Additional Language*, London: London Language and Literacy Unit.

Chapter 3

Barton, D. (1994) *Literacy*, Oxford: Blackwell.

Bhatt, A. and Martin-Jones, M. (1992) 'Whose resource? Minority languages, bilingual learners and language awareness', in N. Fairclough (ed.) *Critical Language Awareness*, Harlow: Longman.

Cameron, D. (2001) *Working with Spoken Discourse*, London: Sage.

Davies, A., Grove, E. and Wilkes, M. (1997) *The Bilingual Interface Project Report: Review of Literature on Acquiring Literacy in a Second Language*, Australian Department of Employment, Education, Training and Youth Affairs.

Hamilton, M. (1996) 'Literacy and adult basic education', in R. Fieldhouse (ed.) *A History of Modern British Adult Education*, Leicester: NIACE.

Hodge, R. and Pitt, K. (2004) '"This is not enough for one's life": perceptions of living and learning English in Blackburn by students seeking asylum and refugee status', *Lancaster Literacy Research Centre Working Papers*, 4.

Hornberger, N. (1994) 'Continua of biliteracy', in B. Ferdman, R-M. Weber and A. Ramirez (eds) *Literacy Across Languages and Cultures*, Albany: State University of New York Press.

ILEA (1990) 'Afro-Caribbean language and literacy project in further and higher education', in *Language and Power*, London: Harcourt Brace Jovanovich.

Lo Bianco, J. (2000) 'Multiliteracies and multilingualism', in B. Cope and M. Kalantzis (eds) *Multiliteracies: Literacy Learning and the Design of Social Futures*, London: Routledge.

McLaughlin, J. (1986) 'Developing writing in English from mother-tongue storytelling', *Language Issues*, 1: 31–34.

Martin-Jones, M. (2000) 'Enterprising women', in M. Martin-Jones and K. Jones (eds) *Multilingual Literacies: Reading and Writing Different Worlds*, Amsterdam: John Benjamins.

Rampton, B. (1991) 'Second language learners in a stratified multilingual setting', *Applied Linguistics*, 12: 229–248.

Richardson, E. (2002) *African-American Literacies*, London: Routledge.

Rivera, K. 1999. 'Popular research and social transformation: a community-based approach to critical pedagogy', *TESOL Quarterly*, 33: 485–500.

Roberts, C. (2003) 'Language, literacy and bilingualism: connecting theory, policy and practice', Paper presented at ESRC Seminar on Literacy, Numeracy and ESOL, Edinburgh.

Romaine, S. (1989) *Bilingualism*, Oxford: Blackwell.

Savitzky, F. (1986) *Language Profile of a West African Student*, London: London Language and Literacy Unit.

Saxena, M. (1994) 'Literacies among the Panjabis in Southall (Britain)', in M. Hamilton, D. Barton and R. Ivanic (eds) *Worlds of Literacy*, Clevedon: Multilingual Matters.

Street, B. (1984) *Literacy in Theory and Practice*, Cambridge: Cambridge University Press.

Chapter 4

American Institutes for Research (2001) 'What Works': A Study of Adult ESL Literacy Students: Research Challenges and Descriptive Findings, Washington, DC: Pelavin Research Centre.

Auerbach, E. (1996) 'Adult ESL/literacy', in *From the Community to the Community: A Guidebook for Participatory Literacy Training*, Mahwah, NJ: Lawrence Erlbaum Associates.

Auerbach, E. (2000) 'Creating participatory learning communities: paradoxes and possibilities', in J. Hall and W. Eggington (eds) *The Sociopolitics of English Language Teaching*, Clevedon: Multilingual Matters.

Bell, J. S. (1993) 'Discussion of Kerfoot and Wrigley: the teacher as bridge between program and practice', *TESOL Quarterly*, 27: 467–475.

Bell, J. S. (1997) *Literacy, Culture and Identity: American University Studies*, New York: Peter Lang.

Burns, A. and de Silva Joyce, H. (eds) (2000) *Teachers' Voices 5: A New Look at Reading Practices*, Sydney: National Center for English Language Teaching and Research, Macquarie University.

Cooke, M. (2000) *Wasted Opportunities: A Case Study of Two ESOL Programmes in a Further Education College in Central London*, Institute of Education, Dissertation for MA TESOL.

Fairclough, N. (2003) *Analysing Discourse: Textual Analysis for Social Research*, London: Routledge.

Gurnah, A. (2000) 'Languages and literacies for autonomy', in M. Martin-Jones and K. Jones (eds) *Multilingual Literacies: Reading and Writing Different Worlds*, Amsterdam: John Benjamins.

Hornberger, N. and Hardman, J. (1994) 'Literacy as cultural practice and cognitive skill:

biliteracy in an ESL class and a GED program', in D. Spencer (ed.) *Adult Biliteracy in the United States*, McHenry, IL: CAL and Delta Systems.

Jessop, M., Lawrence, G. and Pitt, K. (1998) 'Two workshops on critical literacy practice', *RaPAL Bulletin*, 35: 13–16.

Wallace, C. (1992) 'Critical literacy awareness in the EFL classroom', N. Fairclough (ed.) in *Critical Language Awareness*, Harlow, Essex: Longman.

Chapter 5

Bird, S. (1998) *Pushing Learners to Focus on Form*, TESOL, Institute of Education: MA TESOL dissertation.

Bremer, K., Roberts, C., Vasseur, M-T., Simonot, M. and Broeder, P. (1996) *Achieving Understanding: Discourse in Intercultural Encounters*, Harlow, Essex: Longman.

Carter, R. and McCarthy, M. (1997) *Exploring Spoken English*, Cambridge: Cambridge University Press.

Cook, G. (1998) 'The uses of reality: a reply to Ronald Carter', *ELT Journal*, 52: 57–63.

McCarthy, M. and Carter, R. (1995) 'Spoken grammar: what is it and how can we teach it?' *ELT Journal*, 49: 207–18.

Skehan, P. (2001) 'Comprehension and production strategies in language learning', in C. Candlin and N. Mercer (eds) *English Language Teaching in its Social Context*, London: Routledge.

Thornbury, S. (1997) 'Reformulation and reconstruction: tasks that promote "noticing"', *ELT Journal*, 51: 326–335.

Index